HOW TO SURVIVE JUNIOR HIGH BY REALLY TRYING

DAVE AND NETA JACKSON

STORY AND CHARACTERS BASED ON THE
MINI-MOVIE™ OF THE SAME NAME.
STORY BY GEORGE TAWEEL & ROB LOOS,
TELEPLAY BY MARTHA WILLIAMSON

BROADMAN
& HOLMAN
PUBLISHERS

Nashville, Tennessee

Copyright © 1994

BROADMAN & HOLMAN PUBLISHERS

TAWEEL-LOOS & COMPANY ENTERTAINMENT
"The mini-movie™ Studio"

"SMASH" is based on the characters created by
George Taweel & Rob Loos. Story by George Taweel & Rob Loos.
Teleplay written by Shelly Moore. © 1994.
Text illustrations by Anderson Thomas Design, Inc., and
Julian Jackson

Secret Adventures™ and Mister Toaster™ are trademarks of
Broadman & Holman Publishers.
Mini-Movie™ is a registered trademark of
Taweel-Loos & Company Entertainment.
All rights reserved

4240-06
0-8054-4006-2

Dewey Decimal Classification: JF
Subject Heading: HUMAN RELATIONS - FICTION
Library of Congress Card Catalog Number: 94-12997
Printed in the United States of America

Library of Congress Cataloging-in-Publication Data
Jackson, Dave.
    Smash : how to survive jr. high by really trying / by Dave and
Neta Jackson.
        p. cm. — (Secret adventures ; no. 3)
    Summary: Seventh grader Drea Thomas confronts her arch-
enemy Arlene when the students try to raise ten thousand
dollars for the school to keep its extracurricular activities.
    ISBN 0-8054-4006-2 : $4.99
    [1. Cooperativeness—Fiction.   2. Schools—Fiction. 3. Fund
raising—Fiction. 4. Moneymaking projects—Fiction.]
I. Jackson, Neta.   II. Title.   III. Series: Jackson, Dave. Secret
adventures; #3.
PZ7.J132418She   1994
[Fic]—dc20   94-12997
                                                          CIP

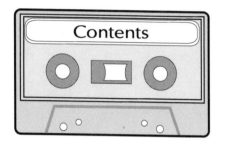

Contents

Live in peace with each other. . . . be patient with everyone. Make sure that nobody pays back wrong for wrong, but always try to be kind to each other and to everyone else.

—1 Thessalonians 5:13b-15, NIV

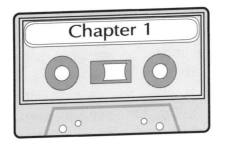

The Day Volleyball Bellyflopped

Oh, no, E.D.! I *would* have to oversleep . . . today of all days! I wanted to get to school early to sign up for the girls' intramural volleyball team . . . and now I'm already running ten minutes late.

Not only that, I must've slept on my hair wrong, because the left side is sticking out funny, and—

— *Click!* —

Sorry about that, E.D. I just ran out of tape and had to scrounge around for another blank cassette. That's one problem with using my Walkman as an *electronic diary*—affectionately known as E.D.—gotta keep a good supply of blank tapes on hand.

Luckily I found one more in my book bag . . . and after Mrs. Long pays me this week for baby-sitting Matt and Rebecca after school, hopefully I can buy some more this weekend. Baby-sitting the principal's kids three days a week really helps my budget, but frankly, the way seventh grade has been going so far, I'm going to need a hundred blank tapes at least!

Well, as long as I got interrupted, I might as well back up and start this diary entry properly—if I can talk and tie my shoes at the same time, that is.

Ahem! It's Wednesday . . . Day 4,865 in the Secret Adventures of Drea Thomas . . . and I'm now running twelve minutes behind schedule! I gotta do something with my hair and jet outta here, E.D., or I'll end up sitting on the sidelines instead of playing volleyball.

Over and out.

— Click! —

It's now after school, E.D., and yours truly is sitting on our front porch watching Matt and Rebecca Long rollerblade on the sidewalk in front of our house. So far, I've only had to scrape Matt off the concrete three times, apply four bandages, and referee five arguments. Amazing record, don't you think?

Weather-wise it turned out to be an absolutely primo fall day here in Hampton Falls, New Jersey . . . but *otherwise*, things haven't been going so good. Not only did I wake up ten minutes late on the very day we were supposed to sign up for extracurricular activities . . . but the bathroom mirror started arguing with me about my hairstyle! Ya see, E.D., I was trying to tame my wild hair with a hairbrush—'course, it didn't help that I was rushing—when my imagination started playing tricks on me . . .

Suddenly my image in the mirror was NOT doing the same thing I was doing!

"Hey!" I protested. "What do you think you're doing? I'm the one fixin' my hair. You're supposed to copy my movements . . . EXACTLY."

"But it doesn't look good that way," said my reflection. "I'm tired of copying your every move—especially when I think I could make your hair look better."

My jaw dropped. This was mutiny! If your own mirror won't cooperate, who will?

"Well, I want it THIS way," I said stubbornly, and gave my hair another flip with the brush.

"No, you don't," argued my reflection. "You really want to brush your hair away from your face . . . like this"—which my image in the mirror proceeded to do with a smug smile.

9

"No . . . I want to wear it down today!"

"Give it up, Drea," said my reflection. "You can't see yourself like I can . . . take my word for it; you need to wear part of your hair up today."

"Forget it!" I said, and stormed out of the bathroom. But out of the corner of my eye, I could see my reflection still back in the mirror, arms crossed, waiting for me to see the error of my ways.

"Oh, all right," I grumbled. "Have it your way . . ."

. . . so I took the time to put part of my hair up in a scrunchee with just the back hanging down . . . which explains why I just barely made it to school as the bell was ringing. *And*, I didn't have time to sign up for girls' volleyball before school and had to wait until lunchtime.

Like I said earlier, E.D., today we were supposed to sign up for extracurricular activities—affectionately known at Hampton Falls Junior High as "E.C.A.'s." What I *really* wanted to sign up for was basketball. Grandpa's been teaching me his hook shot using the hoop on our garage, and . . . well, my shooting percentage isn't exactly NBA stuff, but it's improving. So far, though, all we have is a girl's volleyball team, which is pretty cool, too. But when I got to the gym—

Oh, no! Matt just did another belly flop on the sidewalk!

— *Click!* —

Well, that took more than a hug and a bandage to fix. Matt was wailing that Rebecca tripped him on purpose, but Rebecca insisted it was an accident. You know how it goes, E.D. . . .

"You did so!"

"I did not!"

"Did so."

"Did not."

"Did!"

"Didn't!"

Sigh. If squabbling were an Olympic event open to seven- and nine-year-olds, they'd probably win the gold and silver medals . . . and then fight over who got what!

Anyway, I decided the best cure for big-sister/little-brother brawling was working together on a snack . . . and by the time Rebecca fixed lemonade and Matt put together his peanut-butter-toast-with-banana-slices-and-coconut concoction, Mrs. Long arrived to pick them up.

Just after they left, Mom called from her office at Jamison's Department Store to tell me that Dad has to work late tonight at the college on some Mozart concert thing, so she's going to pick up Chinese food on the way home. Which means I *don't* have to get dinner started, and I *could* dig into my homework . . . but first I wanna finish telling you what happened with the E.C.A. sign-ups, E.D.

As I was saying before Matt tangled with the

sidewalk . . . At lunchtime I headed for the gym to sign up for girls' volleyball. A bunch of other girls were crowded around a sign on the door . . . and one of them was Marcy Mannington.

Now, that was interesting, E.D., because Marcy is rarely seen by herself. She's always following Arlene Blake around like Peter Pan's stitched-on shadow, doing whatever Arlene does. And I *know* Arlene—Miss Popularity at Hampton Falls Junior High, not to mention seventh grade class president—wouldn't be caught dead getting sweaty on a volleyball court. So what was Marcy doing at sign-ups?

Hmm, I thought, *maybe Marcy's got a mind of her own, after all.*

"Hi, Marcy," I said, trying to be friendly.

She looked around nervously . . . and then actually smiled at me. Well, I think it was a smile. Her mouth twitched a little at the corners.

"Gonna sign up for volleyball?" I asked.

She gave a quick little nod. "I hope so," she said, "except . . ." and she tipped her chin toward the sign everyone was looking at. I craned my neck around the heads of the other girls crowded around the gym door and read:

Girls' Volleyball
Sign Up Today
CANCELLED

That was it. Cancelled. *SMASH*. No explanation.

I read it again, hoping that C-A-N-C-E-L-L-E-D really spelled "Postponed" or "Rescheduled" or something. Then I heard a familiar voice shrilling, "Marcy Mannington! What on earth are you doing here?" It was Arlene Blake, with her usual halo of wispy blonde waves, dressed in a pink turtleneck and short skirt with a pink and yellow brocade jacket, looking as if she'd just stepped out of *Sassy* magazine.

"Oh . . . hi, Arlene," Marcy squeaked. "I . . . uh, thought I'd try out for girls' volleyball . . . ya know, just for fun . . . maybe?"

"Huh!" sniffed Arlene, glancing first at me and then at the sign. "It says 'Cancelled' . . . which is just as well, Marcy. Volleyball's not for *you*! Leave all that grunting and panting to the Drea Thomases of the world." And then she looked me up and down, giving a disgusted, once-over glance at my saddle shoes, big shirt, and striped vest. "Come on, Marcy," Arlene finished. "You can sign up for drama club with me."

With that, Arlene put her nose in the air, took Marcy by the arm, and steered her down the hall.

Why is it, E.D., that with just a withering glance and a snide remark, Arlene can make me feel about two inches high? I know she's still mad about me beating her out for the Long kids' baby-sitting gig, but I wish she would give it a rest. That was weeks ago!

I shrugged and turned back to the sign, hoping that a third read would reveal a secret code or something—ya know, where OUT really means IN, YES really means NO, and CANCELLED really means IN PROGRESS—when I heard *another* familiar voice.

"Drea! I've been looking all over for you!" I turned and saw Kimberly Andow—future Broadway star and my best friend—hit her hand to her forehead dramatically, as if she were Aunt Polly catching Tom Sawyer climbing in his bedroom window. "We're supposed to sign up for E.C.A.'s this period, and—"

Kimberly stopped and looked around, as if just realizing we were standing by the gym. "Oh," she said. "You're going to try out for girls' volleyball, huh?"

I nodded at the sign. "*Was* going to," I said glumly. "Looks like it belly flopped."

"Oh," she said again, trying to look suitably sad for me. "But . . . as long as it's been cancelled, you can come sign up for drama club with me!" And she grabbed my arm and started cheerfully down the hall.

"No way, Kimberly," I protested. "I don't *want* to sign up for drama club!" Well . . . I *had* considered it, briefly . . . but knowing that Arlene Blake was *also* signing up for drama club had dropped it down into last place. Having to cope with both my wacky best friend *and* my biggest rival on the same stage would be way too much stress, E.D.

Kimberly breezed on. "Well, if volleyball's cancelled, you have to sign up for *something*." I rolled my eyes and she hastened to add, "Okay, okay . . . just come with me anyway. On the way you can think of something else you want to do."

But when we arrived at the drama room, a bunch of guys and girls were standing around *another* sign. Kimberly and I pushed in closer to see what it said.

Drama Club
Sign-up Today
CANCELLED

Kimberly and I stared at each other. *What* was going on? First girls' volleyball . . . then drama club . . . and later we heard from other kids that *all* the E.C.A. sign-ups had been cancelled—even the African-American Culture Club, which has Bobby Wilson bummed out.

Everyone was buzzing about it, but no one actually *knew* anything. A bunch of us were talking at the bike rack after school, and Bobby Wilson and George Easton wondered if it had anything to do with the "unknown pranksters" who lit firecrackers in the boys' locker room last week.

"Maybe the principal cancelled the E.C.A.'s as a

way to get those guyes to 'fess up," George suggested. "If that's the reason, I for one would gladly tar and feather them!"

Personally, E.D., I think punishing all the junior high students just because a couple of guys acted like jerks would be grossly unfair . . . and besides, that doesn't sound like something Mrs. Long, our principal, would do.

Still, there's got to be *some* explanation. . . . Hey! I just realized I missed a chance to ask Mrs. Long about the E.C.A.'s when she came to pick up Matt and Rebecca a little while ago!

Oh, well . . . I guess it's better to keep my "personal" baby-sitting life separate from my "professional" role as a student anyway.

Oh! Just heard the back door slam . . . must be Mom with the Chinese food . . . and I'm starving! Catch ya later, E.D. Hopefully by tomorrow I'll find out the rest of the story."

— *Click!* —

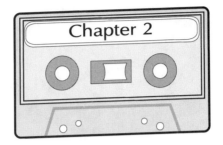

No Money, Honey

Testing . . . testing . . . okay, guess this is working. It's still a little awkward trying to record my electronic diary and ride my bike at the same time, but I'll get the hang of it one of these days.

It's Thursday morning . . . Day 4,866 in the Secret Adventures of Drea Thomas . . . and my watch says . . .

Suddenly the watch-face on my neon-colored watch—that looks like a "Swatch" to ordinary mortals—goes into a quick spin, and when it stops, it's showing a twenty-four-hour clock face instead of the normal twelve numbers . . . and a pro-

grammed voice says, "At the tone, the time will be oh-seven-forty-five hundred hours" . . .

. . . and my Western Flyer and I are on our way to school to learn "the rest of the story" about our E.C.A.'s.

But if you were a *video* diary, E.D., I could show you what a gorgeous day it is! Fall is my fave time of year here in Hampton Falls . . . all the leaves are turning yellow and red and orange, and they flutter like a zillion flags against the sky, which today is a brilliant blue. Some of them are starting to fall already . . . and you know what that means! Grandpa Ben will soon be saying, "Oh, Drea! How's my favorite granddaughter? Say, why don't we spend some quality time together . . . raking leaves!"

Yep, I'll bet my next baby-sitting pay he'll figure a way to get a rake in my hands by the end of the week!

Well, gotta sign off for now, E.D. There's the

school up ahead . . . Hey, Cristan! What'zappenin'?
— *Click!* —

Now, what was *that* all about?

As I pulled up to the bike rack, I yelled "Hi!" to Cristan Cantor, who was walking with some eighth grade guy . . . but just then the dweeb she was with jerked his thumb at my bike and said, "Hey, where'd you get that piece of junk—at a garage sale? Looks like a prop for 'Leave It to Beaver' reruns!" Then he laughed—and Cristan laughed, too, and walked off with him, without even saying hi!

Oh, well. Got more important things to worry about, I guess. Hey . . . there's George! At least *he* appreciates the difference between just an "old-fashioned" bike and a real "classic."

Hey, George! Wait up! . . . Over and out, E.D.
— *Click!* —

It's twenty-thirty hundred hours—that's 8:30 P.M. to civilians—and I'm back home in my attic bedroom staring at a pile of homework that would make the Leaning Tower of Pisa topple over . . . but I'm having a hard time concentrating after what happened today.

I mean, we all knew *something* was up when the E.C.A. sign-ups were cancelled yesterday. But we didn't know exactly what had happened until today when the principal called a special assembly.

First of all, Mrs. Long apologized for cancelling the E.C.A. sign-ups so abruptly yesterday—but she said that she was in budget meetings all day with the school board and so couldn't give us an explanation.

After her apology, I thought I heard a big sigh of relief somewhere in the auditorium—probably the guys who set off the firecrackers in the boys' locker room, who just realized there might be some other reason the E.C.A.'s got cancelled, and that maybe 547 junior high students weren't going to tar and feather them after all!

Anyway . . . then Mrs. Long told us the school board had to cut ten thousand dollars from its budget this year, and they sliced it from—you guessed it—the extracurricular activities. That means no drama club or Spanish club or computer club . . . no cheerleaders . . . no student newspaper . . . no field trips . . . no girls' *volleyball* . . . you know, E.D., all the *good* stuff!

At that point, near-pandemonium broke out. Kids were angry about losing their favorite activities . . . some of them even started shouting at Mrs. Long. The teachers quickly took us all back to our classes, and somehow we made it till last period . . . but all day you could tell kids were really upset, including yours truly—

Riiiiinng.

—Just a minute, E.D. . . . gotta get the phone.
— *Click!* —

That was Kimberly, totally bummed at losing the drama club. She said her acting career at Hampton Falls Junior High has been cruelly crushed for lack of a mere ten thousand bucks. And as far as she's concerned, drama shouldn't be considered an *extra*curricular activity, but part of the regular curriculum—

Riiiiinng.

Sorry, E.D. Phone again . . .

Starship Enterprise . . . Doctor Crusher speaking . . . oh, hi, Bobby. Wait a sec—let me shut off my Walkman.

— *Click!* —

That was Bobby Wilson, E.D., one of our star soccer players. He just realized that no E.C.A.'s means there aren't going to be any more away soccer games. The money for the buses for away games were in the E.C.A. budget. Now *he's* all bummed out—

Riiiiinng.

What *is* it with the phone!?

Long distance operator, all circuits are jammed . . . hey, hey, calm down, George! It's me, Drea!

— *Click!* —

Back again, E.D. . . . poor George.

Now, George Easton's generally a laid-back dude, E.D. He and Bobby are best buddies, and even though he ranks right up there with Bobby as one of our school's best soccer players, he *usually* keeps his feet on the ground—so I knew he was upset when his voice started squeaking between bass and soprano, babbling something about just realizing that the field trip to the annual Science Fair will probably have to be called off. *Field trips* were in the E.C.A. budget, too.

It's kinda strange, E.D. . . . I never paid any attention before to school boards or budget stuff. Now, suddenly, it's already Day Two of a major school budget crisis, and the decisions they're making hit really close to home. Everybody wants to get his or her own favorite E.C.A. back, but everybody thinks it's somebody else's responsibility. Seems like the students are the ones affected most . . . maybe we ought to—

Riiiiinng.

I don't believe this! Who's calling this time? Guess there's only one way to find out . . .

— *Click!* —

Well, I shoulda known. That was Grandpa Ben, E.D., inviting me to—as I expected—rake leaves with him on Saturday! Are we surprised?

I shouldn't complain. Grandpa's cool. Ever since

he retired from the railroad, he's lived in an apartment where he doesn't have a yard to putter around in . . . says he misses it . . . so, he takes it out on our yard and garden, which Mom and Dad appreciate a lot. Mom's job as marketing director for Jamison's Department Store and Dad's job as music prof at the local junior college don't leave much time for keeping up with the yard around this humongous old house—much less raising vegetables and flowers! But the first time Mom took a bite of one of Grandpa's juicy, sweet, vine-ripened tomatoes, she said she would never be satisfied with a store-bought tomato again!

'Course, I don't think Mom realizes all the *work* it takes to produce a home-grown tomato. But Grandpa seems to think *somebody* around the Thomas household should learn the gardening secrets passed down from his dad, my great-grandfather Thomas.

Which means me.

Oh, well. I kinda like it . . . most of the time. Grandpa's the best . . . in fact, maybe he'll have some ideas about this budget crisis thing. The whole thing just doesn't seem fair!

Sigh. Guess I better do my homework . . . although I suppose I could always try a new excuse for not getting it done, like, "It's the school board's fault . . . they cut out all our E.C.A.'s. and everybody's upset, so my phone was ringing all evening . . ." Sounds better than claiming that the dog ate it.

Naaah, I don't think so.

Over and out, E.D.

— Click! —

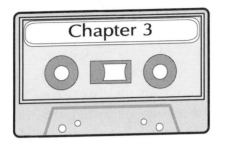

Chapter 3

Friday Night with Wolfgang

G'morning, E.D.

I've got a few minutes before I have to leave for school, so thought I'd enjoy the peace out here on the back porch while I eat my toast. Hmm . . . there are more leaves on the ground than I thought. Guess Grandpa and I have our work cut out for us tomorrow.

Oh . . . I better identify date and time. This is an electronic *diary*, after all.

It's Friday . . . Day 4,867 in the Secret Adventures of Drea Thomas . . . also Day Three of "Our School Budget Crisis"—which will be known from now on as O.S.B.C.—and . . . hey! Can you hear that, E.D.? That boom-boom-brassy sound? That's the marching band practicing on the college campus where Dad is a music prof.

Speaking of my dad . . . he's in one of his weird moods again. Well, not a "mood" exactly . . . it's just that he gets all involved in these projects he dreams up, and he walks around muttering to himself or humming little tunes or bringing home a new instrument-of-the-week.

Like this morning . . . Mom had already gone to work, and a few minutes ago I was making a quick piece of toast in our antique toaster when Dad wandered into the kitchen, frowning thoughtfully at some music he was holding in his hand. Without even looking up, he fished in the fruit bowl for a banana, peeled it with his teeth, took a big bite, and then went wandering away.

"Dad . . . watch out!" I warned, just before he ran into the doorpost leading into the dining room.

He turned around, looking a little dazed and sheepish; then he grinned at me and waved the music in his hand. "Moshart conshirt," he grinned, his mouth still full of banana . . . which, when translated, means that he's preparing for the annual Mozart concert . . . I think.

When I was sure Dad was going to be all right, I turned back to rescue my toast from our unpredictable ancient toaster . . . but I was too late. Smoke was already rising from the two slots on top of the toaster, so I banged on the side handle to pop up my toast before it set a new burn record . . .

As I peered into the shiny chrome sides of the toaster, my reflection was all distorted—little eyes, big nose—and in a blink I was staring eyeball to eyeball with my friend, Mr. Toaster.

"Hey!" said the toaster, wiggling his side handle tenderly. "Careful with the merchandise! How do you think I've lasted this long, anyway? Not by someone banging away at my sensitive handles." And Mr. Toaster eyed first one handle, and then the other, to make sure they were both okay.

I leaned on the counter. " 'Careful with the merchandise,' eh?" I said, unimpressed. "I could say the same thing about my toast. Aren't you supposed to TOAST it? Not CHARBROIL it!" And I held up the piece of black toast.

"Complaining again, are we?" sniffed the toaster. "What do you expect when you don't pay attention? You're supposed to watch while I'm toasting, and then pop it up—gently—when it's the way you like it."

"Me?" I said. "You're the toaster. That's your job!"

"Hey, haven't you heard about cooperation?" asked the toaster. "I toast . . . you watch."

"Oh, right," I said, rolling my eyes. *Like I had time to baby-sit the toaster every time I wanted a piece of toast . . .*

. . . but just to be safe, I did it Mr. Toaster's way and actually got an edible piece of toast to munch—

Yikes! It's time to hit the road, Jack, or I'm gonna be late to school!

Over and out, E.D.

— Click! —

I don't get it, E.D. Why do some people talk one way to your face and another way behind your back? (At least when my reflection in the bathroom mirror gets smart with me, it's to my face!) You see . . .

Oh. Forgot my I.D. check . . . it's still Day Three of O.S.B.C. and I just got home from school. I baby-sit on Friday, so Rebecca and Matt will be showing up here any minute.

Anyway, as I was saying . . . as Kimberly and I were walking down the hall at school today, Cristan Canter waved at me and called out, "Hi, Drea! Isn't it awful about the E.C.A.'s?" . . . as if yesterday she hadn't totally ignored me, and even laughed at my bike with that super-dweeb eighth grader.

But I decided maybe I was being too sensitive—especially if Cristan was as upset about losing the E.C.A.'s as George and Bobby and the rest. At a time like this, we need to stick together, ya know. So I said, "Yeah, Cristan, it's a bummer." Then I remembered something. "Say . . . isn't your mother on the school board? Maybe you could ask her if a delegation of students could come talk to the board or something—"

"Uh . . . I don't know, Drea," Cristan said, backing up a step. "We're just junior high kids . . . I'm sure the board knows what it's doing . . ."

She hurried off . . . and later Kimberly told me she overheard Marcy Mannington tell Arlene that Cristan had told her that Drea Thomas just has to get involved in everything.

Man, am I steamed! I thought Cristan was my friend! At least, I'm *her* friend when it's time for her annual birthday bash and she needs help planning the entertainment.

It's bad enough having to put up with sarcastic remarks from Arlene Blake all the time without wondering what my so-called friends are saying when I'm not around—

Uh-oh, I hear Matt and Rebecca coming in the back door . . . squabbling, as usual. Better cut and run, E.D.

— Click! —

Whew! Finally alone again, E.D. What is it with those two? When I got down to the kitchen, Matt had made a beeline for the radio on the counter and was trying to tune it to WWEN, all the while fending off Rebecca, who was insisting he had to do his homework first.

"I just want to hear the next Code-Buster clue," Matt said stubbornly, twirling the dial.

"Oh, right," Rebecca said, rolling her eyes. She turned to me with exaggerated patience. "Matt thinks he can play the Code-Buster game on WWEN and win lots of money." She turned back to Matt. "Don't forget: you're only in first grade and don't even know how to *spell* yet."

"So?" said Matt, sticking out his lip. "I like puzzles."

I kinda agree with Rebecca. Matt seems pretty young to be playing those radio contests. I mean, half the state of New Jersey is probably trying to figure out that "Code-buster" thing! But I didn't say anything. Instead I just motioned with my head for Rebecca to come upstairs with me, and we left Matt kneeling on a kitchen chair, still wearing his blue and red baseball cap, his ear glued to the radio.

A few minutes later he pounded up the stairs to my attic bedroom. "How do you spell *dolphin*?" he panted.

"See?" said Rebecca, looking up from her home-work. "I told you he couldn't spell."

"Didn't ask you," Matt pouted.

"Did too."

"Did not."

"Did."

"Didn't!"

"STOP!" I shouted.

Honestly, E.D., sometimes I wonder why I ever agreed to baby-sit my principal's kids after school. Then I remember: oh, yeah, the money. And I have to admit: I really do like having them around . . . most of the time. It's kinda like having a younger sister and little brother . . . in fact, now that I think of it, it's *exactly* like that—especially when they're picking on each other!

Anyway. I told Matt how to spell *dolphin* and we made it through the rest of the afternoon without any more fights. Mrs. Long just picked them up . . . before she left I worked up the courage to ask her if there was any hope of the school board reversing its decision about the E.C.A.'s, but she just shook her head. "I don't think so, Drea," she said. "They're not trying to be mean; there just isn't any money."

Which makes it even more depressing. I mean, if the board just didn't like the *idea* of extracurricular activities, then we students could demand a hearing, tell them how important E.C.A.'s are to us, make a case for their educational value . . . all that sort of stuff. But what can a bunch of seventh and eighth graders do about $10,000 that doesn't exist?

Oh, well. Mom and Dad should be home soon. Mom didn't tell me to start anything for dinner . . . but I think I saw a jar of spaghetti sauce in the pantry. If we've got a box of spaghetti noodles, I'm in business. But we need something else to go with it . . . hmm, I wonder how Mom and Dad would go for an exotic salad?

Catch ya later, E.D.

— *Click!* —

It's now after dinner and I'm waiting for Kimberly . . . she's supposed to pick me up, and we're going to go hang out at the mall for a while tonight—you know, drown our sorrows with a little Friday night window shopping.

Except . . . it's starting to rain. Bummer.

Anyway, E.D., the spaghetti was okay, but the "exotic" salad I concocted didn't go over so well. Kinda surprised me, 'cause I know both Mom and Dad like chocolate fondue. But for some reason they just stared at my tropical fruit salad with chocolate fudge sauce over it. And it even had kiwi fruit in it! Oh, well. Ya win some and lose some.

But tonight I found out the junior high isn't the only school having money problems in Hampton Falls. Dad was looking pretty glum when he came home—he said the college administration is threatening to cancel the annual Mozart concert after this year. They told him, "It doesn't produce enough revenue"—which translated means money—"to justify the expense" . . . or something like that.

So Dad, as head of the music department, is trying to think of exciting ways to publicize the concert and prove them wrong.

"Help me out, Drea," he said. (Actually, E.D., he was begging.) "You've got a good imagination. I need some ideas that will arouse the curiosity of the musically indifferent, and lure the rock-blasted college student into the concert hall."

Poor Dad . . . I wish I could help him out. But we junior high students are losing *all* our extracurricular activities—not just one concert—and none of us have a clue what to do about that. But I had to say something, so off the top of my head, I suggested, "Well, there's a docu-drama or something about Mozart on TV tonight—you know, the educational channel. Maybe it would give you some ideas."

Dad's eyebrows went up. "Hmmm," he said, running his hands through his hair like he does when he's thinking hard. "Hmm . . . depends . . ."

Mom jumped in. "Jim, it's worth a try . . . and it might spark some ideas."

So he and Mom went out to get some popcorn to go with the program. Hope it works . . . right now, I wish someone would give *me* an idea what we students could do to save our E.C.A.'s.—

Aiiiiieeee! What was that?

— *Click!* —

That was the loudest clap of thunder I've ever heard in my whole life, E.D.! Scared my bow tie right out of its knot. Hope none of our trees got struck by lightening—*help!* There's another one! And now it's raining buckets—

Riiiinnng.

There's the phone . . . bet it's Kimberly . . .

— *Click!* —

I was right. She said *no way* is her mom going to drive us to the mall in this storm! So . . . guess I'm fated to stay home and watch that movie about good ol' A.W.M. with Mom and Dad.

Can you believe it, E.D.? It's Friday night, the night all teenagers look forward to all week, and I'm gonna be hanging out with my *parents* and *Wolfie Mozart* . . . this, on top of a week where we lost our E.C.A.'s at school, Rebecca and Matt have set a new record for arguing, and people I thought I had figured out—like Marcy Mannington and Cristan Canter—are *not* being predictable. *Sigh.*

— *Click!* —

P.S. to Day Three . . .

Mom and Dad got home okay, but they were soaking wet just getting from the car into the house!

The docu-drama was great. I'd forgotten how brilliant Mozart was, even as a child. Or maybe Mozart went over my head when I had Music Appreciation in sixth grade. But right in the middle of the show, Dad jumped up and yelled, "I've got it!"

"What? What?" I said. "Chicken pox? Bubonic plague?"

But Dad just grabbed me in a big bear hug—spilling my bowl of popcorn all over the rug—and danced me around the room. "Thank you, Drea!" he crowed. "I've got an idea how to publicize the Mozart concert!

"Uh . . . that's great!" I said. "What's your idea?"

"No . . . no, I can't tell you yet," he said vaguely. "I've got to figure out how to pull it off first. *Then* I'll tell you."

So, now Dad will be happy and mysterious and distracted and bumping into things for a few days.

According to my watch it's only . . . hmm . . . twenty-two hundred hours, but it's still raining monkeys and elephants, which makes getting into bed with a good book seem like a really great idea.

Hmm . . . it's a good thing I like the sound of rain, 'cause up here in my bedroom under the eaves, it feels like I'm in Noah's Ark riding out the Big Flood.

G'night, E.D.

— *Click!* —

Double P.S. I bet this means my "date" with Grandpa is off for tomorrow. I mean, not even *Grandpa* would rake leaves in the rain!

— *Click!* —

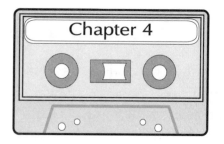

Operation Band Aid

Can you believe this, E.D.? Grandpa and the weatherman must be in cahoots, 'cause the sun is out and sucking up rain puddles like a Slurpee this morning! I still thought it might be too wet to rake leaves . . . but no, Grandpa called and said he'd come over around noon, and by that time it ought to be fine.

Not only that, but the storm last night knocked more leaves off the trees. The yard is ankle deep already. We'll be raking till midnight! . . . which would *not* be cool, 'cause Kimberly *also* called and wants to go to the mall later today since we couldn't go last night.

Oh, well. Guess I should clean my room and get

my laundry started . . .

Catch ya later, E.D.

— Click! —

According to my mighty morphing watch, it's now . . . hmm, fifteen-hundred hours . . . okay, okay, three o'clock . . . Saturday afternoon . . . Day 4,868 . . . and I'm waiting for Kimberly to get here. Believe it or not, Grandpa and I got the yard done in two hours! What a team! Not only that, he gave me a great idea! . . . but I'm getting ahead of myself.

Grandpa arrived with a couple of pairs of gardening gloves and a couple of big pumpkins to put on the back porch—they'll make great jack-o'-lanterns in a couple weeks. I was glad to see the gloves—my hands usually grow blisters just *looking* at a rake! But I have to admit those monster pumpkins he brought make the ones I'm trying to grow in the garden look like *pygmy* pumpkins.

"Don't worry, Drea," Grandpa said, noticing me comparing pumpkins. "There's other things you can do with pumpkins besides carve scary faces on em." And he rubbed his stomach and chuckled. That's Grandpa, E.D. . . . I have a feeling I'm going to get a lesson in pie making next!

Anyway, as we started in on the yard, I noticed that the chrysanthemums, zinnias, and marigolds Grandpa planted last spring were even thicker and brighter after last night's rain, a whole rainbow of different colors, looking sorta like a United Nations of Flowers or something . . .

. . . but as I looked closer, the mums seemed to be whispering among themselves, looking sideways at the dwarf marigolds and snickering.

"Hey, wait a minute," I said, "not you flowers, too! I thought only junior high kids cut each other down."

A particularly gorgeous spider mum shook off the last remaining droplets of rain. "Well, we think this flower bed would be stylin' if it were all spider mums like us, and not those . . . those pee-wee marigolds who probably haven't even reached puberty yet."

"You should talk!" a marigold piped up. "Whoever heard of a name like SPIDER MUM!? Makes me think of creepy, *crawly insects . . ."*

Giggling erupted among the marigolds.

"On the other hand," the fiesty little marigold went on, "the name MARIGOLD has a bright, elegant sound, don't you think, Drea?"

"Oh, no, you don't," I protested. "I'm not going to get involved in your petty quarrels. It's bad enough refereeing Rebecca and Matt when they're squabbling."

"Well, if I had my way," a tall zinnia spoke up from the back of the flower bed, "I'd put the mari-golds over THERE . . ." —the zinnia nodded toward the far fence— *". . . and the chrysanthemums over THERE . . ."* —the zinnia nodded toward the ga-rage— *". . . and then we zinnias would get a little breathing room around here instead of all being crammed in the back of the flower bed like this."*

There was a murmuring of agreement among all the zinnias.

"I don't believe this," I muttered. "This flower bed is as bad as a school full of seventh and eighth graders . . ."

Just then Grandpa interrupted my little debate with the flower bed, and I realized I was talking out loud.

"What's that you're saying, Drea?" he asked, sitting down in a lawn chair for a breather. "Some-times my hearing tunes out on me."

"Oh . . . uh . . . nothing, Grandpa." I looked at the flower bed. The spider mums, marigolds, and zinnias were nodding lazily in the warm October breeze, a picture of perfect harmony.

I sighed and leaned on my rake. "It's just that . . . I'm tired of junior high, Grandpa."

Grandpa looked at me in surprise. "Oh? I thought you liked your school."

I shrugged. "Oh, the school's okay, I guess . . . it's the people going there that are driving me nuts."

"Oh," Grandpa said.

I could have dropped it . . . why dump on Grandpa? But suddenly all the frustrations of the week just kind of boiled over. "Everybody's competing with each other. One minute you think somebody's your friend, and the next minute they go and talk about you behind your back." I told him about what happened with Cristan Canter. "And that's not counting people like Arlene Blake who don't even pretend to be my friend," I added.

Grandpa nodded knowingly. "I think you're gonna find that all through life, Drea."

I rolled my eyes. "You're not very encouraging, Grandpa." I raked together another pile of leaves, scooped them up between my hands and the rake, and stuffed them into the big, plastic leaf bag.

"Besides," I said, "that's not all that's going on at school." Then I told him it was Day Four of O.S.B.C., and that all our extracurricular activities got cut out of the school budget, and everybody was upset about their own favorite E.C.A. getting the chop and looking around for somebody to blame, but nobody was actually *doing* anything about it.

Grandpa leaned back in the lawn chair, thinking. "You know, Drea," he said, "what you said kinda reminds me of a passage in the Bible I learned when I was about your age . . ."

I stopped raking. Grandpa remembers more Bible verses than anyone I know—part of the heritage he got from his preacher father.

"Let's see," Grandpa said, "I think it went: 'Live in peace . . . be patient . . . make sure that nobody pays back wrong for wrong . . .'" Grandpa scratched his chin. "But above all else," he added, ". . . 'be kind to each other and to everyone else.'"

I thought about that. Did those things describe anybody I knew?

It was almost like Grandpa read my thoughts. "'Course . . . those are the last things most people want to do," he added.

I rolled my eyes and dumped another armful of leaves into the plastic bag. "Yep . . . that's junior high!" *And,* I thought to myself, *there's not much cooperation between a certain pair of kids I baby-sit for, either!*

Grandpa chuckled knowingly.

We raked for a while longer, and as we were

filling the last leaf bag, Grandpa said, "Ya know, Drea, I've been thinking . . . ten thousand dollars is a lot of money, but if you break that down into smaller amounts . . ."

At Grandpa's words, it was like a gong went off inside my head . . . like those "See If You Can Ring the Bell!" contests at county fairs. My rake morphed into a large mallet, but it was so heavy I could barely pick it up . . . then suddenly a dozen other arms and hands joined in from somewhere and we all picked up the mallet and . . . SMASH! . . . that little black puck went soaring up the bell tower, moving faster and faster toward a big red $10,000, and then . . . BOIIINNNG! Stars and little tweety birds went spinning around at the sweet sound of success!

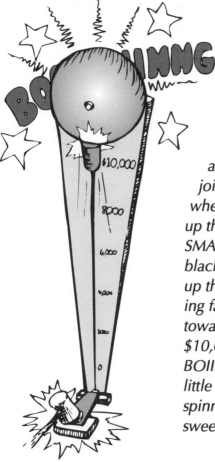

"That's it, Grandpa!" I shouted, giving him a big hug. "If we all cooperate, and each raise *part* of the money . . . Uh, are we done raking leaves? I gotta go call Kimberly!"

We were, and I did. "Kimberly," I said, when she answered the phone, "forget the mall . . . we've got more important things to do!"

"What are you talking about, Drea Thomas?" she said. "What could be more important than going to the mall?"

I finally convinced her that if we wanted to get our E.C.A.'s back, we should act NOW. So she's coming over—oughta be here any second . . . Wow, am I prophetic or what? I think that's Mrs. Andow dropping Kimberly off now.

Gotta sign off, E.D.—here's hoping my idea will help save our E.C.A.'s!

— *Click!* —

Back again, E.D.

It didn't take long for Kimberly to get excited about rescuing the drama club from oblivion. She liked my idea of forming a "Save the E.C.A.'s!" committee.

"You're right, Drea," she said, pacing up and down the braided rug in my room. "I mean, if people can band together to save the rain forests from extinction or . . . or give concerts like 'Farm

Aid,' why can't junior high students band together to save our E.C.A.'s?"

I was sitting on my bed in an old flannel shirt and jeans—it *is* Saturday, after all, when I usually go "grungie"—while Kimberly paced the floor in her big, pastel sweater, stretch pants, and ankle boots, which, admittedly, looked great with her exotic, long dark hair. Dad says we're a perfect example of how "opposites" attract!

"Hmm," I said, "*band* together . . . to *aid* the E.C.A.'s . . . hey! We could call our committee Operation Band Aid!"

That cracked us up. At least now we have a name for our idea . . . but once we quit laughing, we realized we needed more people on our committee to brainstorm fund-raising ideas. I'm supposed to call George and Bobby and see if they can get together at my house Sunday night—that's tomorrow—and hopefully come up with a plan to raise money . . . *lots* and *lots* of money!

Over and out, E.D.

— *Click!* —

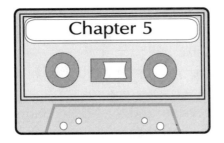

Assault on Mount Megabucks

Check-in time, E.D.

It's Sunday night . . . Day 4,869 in the Secret Adventures of Drea Thomas . . . otherwise known as Day Five of "Our School Budget Crisis" . . . and Kimberly, George, and Bobby just left after our first Operation Band Aid committee meeting. All weekend my mind has been buzzing with fund-raising schemes, and I was really excited to get the committee together and begin making some plans . . . but I think it's going to be tougher than I thought.

First of all, we couldn't agree on a fund-raising project. George thought it'd be great for the soccer team to sell hoagies at the next game—which isn't till next Saturday. But Kimberly turned up her nose.

"Hoagies!" she said. "Only jocks and rednecks eat hoagies. All that ham and summer sausage and drippy dressing—it's gotta be a . . . a colossal cholesterol catastrophe!"

Just then my dad poked his head into the kitchen, where we were gorging ourselves on popcorn and sodas around the kitchen table.

"Did I hear someone say hoagies?" he asked hopefully. "Got one to spare?"

We all stared at him . . . and the urge to laugh was almost primal. Kimberly turned red in the face, but somehow she managed to stammer, "Oh . . . no, Mr. Thomas. We were just discussing fund-raising ideas. But we've . . . uh . . . got lots of popcorn." And she held out the popcorn bowl.

"Oh," said Dad, obviously disappointed. "No, that's okay." And his head disappeared again.

George leaned toward Kimberly. "*See?*" he hissed.

Now, I have to admit that hoagies aren't exactly my favorite sandwich, E.D.—if you can call an over-stuffed, foot-long loaf of bread a "sandwich"—but obviously some people crave 'em, like Bill Cosby . . . and my dad.

But Kimberly was ready to move on. "Well, I've got a *great* idea," she said, standing up and putting both hands on the table, like a politician making a point. "My mom and her friends do this all the time, and make lots of money for different charities.

Are you ready?"

We all nodded hopefully.

"A white elephant sale!" she said.

It was Bobby's turn to choke on his popcorn. "A white elephant WHAT?" he said.

George poked Bobby in the side with his elbow. "A sale on white elephants, dork!" he said in mock seriousness. "She's obviously discovered that we have a shortage of white elephants in Hampton Falls. I know I haven't seen one around here in . . . oh, must be a year, at least!"

It must have been that remark about not seeing any white elephants around Hampton Falls that triggered it, E.D. Because as George and Bobby were joking around, they started to morph right before my eyes . . .

The boys' noses grew long, wrinkled, and rubbery-looking. Their ears stretched wa-a-ay out, large and floppy. Where Bobby and George had been, now sat two enormous, chalky white elephants, scrunched tightly into our kitchen chairs. One sported a neat, black, box haircut on top of his head; the other had brown, wavy hair hanging in his eyes. Both were wearing too small Hampton Falls T-shirts with "SALE" stickers stuck all over them and eating hoagies like popcorn.

"Hey, Georgie," smirked the one with the box haircut, his mouth full of bread and sausage. "How

much you selling for?"

"Don't worry, Bobby. I wouldn't take less than
. . . a dollar a pound."

"Hey! That's good!" the other elephant snorted.
"At three-and-a-half tons . . . that's seven thousand
dollars! A real bargain."

The two elephants lifted their trunks and trum-
peted a few blasts. "All right! . . . We'll save the
day! . . . Seven thousand is pretty good pay! . . .
Now pass me another hoagie."

I blinked . . . and there sat George and Bobby, once again looking like normal junior high guys— 'course I use the word "normal" loosely, E.D.— stuffing their mouths with popcorn and washing it down with soda. I glanced at them nervously, but they were oblivious to my crazy imagination.

Kimberly was leaning against the refrigerator, obviously not amused. "Are you guys through making smart remarks about my idea?" she said, folding her arms and rolling her eyes impatiently.

I tried to steer the conversation back to the problem at hand.

"But, Kimberly," I said, "doesn't a 'white elephant' mean something that somebody can't get rid of? As in, 'That lamp is a white elephant— nobody wants it!' "

"Ah-Aha!" said Kimberly. "That's just the point. One person's 'white elephant' is another person's treasure. We get person #1 to donate it for free, but then we sell it to person #2 and keep the money. *Voila!* One hundred percent profit." Kimberly threw up her hands, struck a pose, and waited for the applause.

Bobby sighed. "I don't know, Kimberly. Sounds kinda risky to me. We might just get stuck with all those 'white elephants.' But . . . *my* idea is a sure thing. A car wash! Everybody wants to get their car washed. I've done it before for Boy Scouts and our church youth group—you can make lots of money!"

George groaned. "Sounds like a lot of *work* to me."

I was beginning to feel frustrated. "Well, of course it's going to take work. Ten thousand dollars isn't going to just come floating down from the sky."

"Don't remind me," George said. "Rerun what you said about how easy it's gonna be to raise fifty or a hundred bucks . . . and how all those fifties and hundreds will magically add up . . . eventually."

Kimberly turned to me. "We haven't heard your idea yet, Drea."

I thought they'd never ask. "Well, actually," I said mysteriously, "I *was* thinking about all ten thousand dollars, and how we have 547 students at Hampton Falls Junior High . . ."

I paused.

"So?" said Kimberly, George, and Bobby.

"Well," I said, getting out my pad of paper, "if you divide 547 into ten thousand, you get . . ." I quickly scribbled some long division, ". . . approximately $18.28."

Kimberly, George, and Bobby just looked at me. "So?" they echoed again, like a Greek chorus.

"Don't you see? If we charged every single student—say, twenty dollars—to come to school for just one day, know what we'd have?

"Yeah," Bobby snickered. "Five hundred and forty-seven absentees."

George grinned in agreement.

"No!" I said. "We'd have ten thousand dollars to hand to the school board and we'd get our E.C.A.'s back" —I snapped my fingers— "just like that!"

Kimberly shook her head. "It wouldn't work."

"Why not?" I asked, looking at George and Bobby for support. But they didn't look very enthused either.

"Kids don't like to pay somethin' for nothin'," Bobby said.

"What do you mean, *nothing*?" I argued. "They'd get the extracurricular activities back!"

"But not all the kids sign up for E.C.A.'s," Kimberly pointed out. "And if they had to pay twenty dollars for doing it, even fewer would sign up."

"Well . . ." I conceded, "but if the kids who *do* sign up for E.C.A.'s each paid twenty dollars . . ." I mentally lowered my expectations. "Five thousand . . . or three . . . or even one thousand would be a good start."

Now George shook his head. "Then we'd have parents upset about *un*equal opportunity," he said. "It would look like the school offered extracurricular activities only to kids who could afford it."

SMASH.

In my brain I saw my brilliant idea shatter into itty bitty pieces. I hated to admit it, but George had a point.

I slumped in my chair. Two minutes ago getting ten thousand dollars had seemed so quick . . . so easy . . . so painless.

Kimberly plopped back in her chair. "Now what?" she asked, heaving a big sigh. "We still haven't come up with an idea we all like."

"Yeah," I admitted, "but . . . ." My mind started spinning again. "We *do* have three ideas—and maybe that's even better! It's just like Jack Sprat and his wife . . . ."

Kimberly, George, and Bobby just looked at me.

"Jack Sprat?" said Kimberly.

"His wife?" said George.

"Mr. and Mrs. Sprat?" said Bobby.

My three best buddies, talented in so many other areas, were *obviously* culturally deprived when it came to nursery rhymes.

"Yeah. You know . . ." and I recited my old Mother Goose favorite . . .

> *Jack Sprat could eat no fat,*
> *His wife could eat no lean.*
> *And so betwixt the two of them,*
> *They licked the platter clean!*

Bobby looked at Kimberly and George, then back at me.

"Drea," he said slowly, as though talking to a small child. "What does licking platters have to do with raising money for our E.C.A.'s?"

Honestly, E.D., they were so dense. "*Some* people—like my dad—will buy hoagies and actually eat them (we hope) ... *some* people hate hoagies, but *will* spend money on somebody else's junk (sorry, Kimberly) ... and *some* people won't buy someone else's junk but *will* pay us to wash their dirty cars," I explained patiently.

I could almost see little lightbulbs going off over Kimberly's, George's, and Bobby's heads.

"Oh!" said Kimberly. "You mean—"

"Right," I said. "We'll do all three fund-raisers! That way we'll give everybody *something* they like ..."

So, E.D., George is gonna see if he can get the soccer team to sell hoagies at the next game, Kimberly is gonna organize the white elephant sale, and Bobby is gonna get a crew of volunteers to do a car wash this weekend in the school parking lot.

So, E.D., we finally got it together long enough to launch our first assault on Mount Megabucks! Tomorrow I'll get the principal's okay on our Operation Band Aid committee to help make it official ... but right now I'm gonna make a big chart to record our progress toward that ten thousand dollar goal.

Hmm ... wonder how much of my computer paper I'd have to tape together to make a six-foot high chart—

Come in! . . . Oh, hi, Mom. . . . Study for what exams?

— Click! —

Oh, no, E.D.! Mom just reminded me I have quarter exams this coming week! I'll never be able to work on these fundraisers if I have to study for exams *and* baby-sit the Long kids after school.

Groan. Nothing like running into a brick wall before we even get started.

Sigh . . . Mom says I better get started reviewing my study sheets. So, over and out for now, E.D. But the way things are going, the world may creep into a new ice age before we raise enough money to get our E.C.A.'s back.

— Click! —

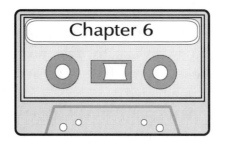

Bigtime Shortfall

Dear E.D. . . . let me introduce myself. My name is Drea Thomas and once upon a time I had good intentions of keeping up with my electronic diary once a day.

But my last entry was Sunday . . . it's now Saturday morning . . . Day 4,875 in the Secret Adventures of Drea Thomas and Day Seven in Drea's Marathon Study Week . . . but I think I survived my first exams at Hampton Falls Junior High. At least I'm still breathing.

It's also Day Eleven of O.S.B.C. . . . and the only thing I've accomplished so far toward our goal of raising ten thousand dollars is making a few signs advertising the hoagie sale at the soccer game today. I thought I could count on Rebecca and Matt to paint up a storm—they usually love doing art projects—but they spent so much time arguing that we ended up with exactly two posters saying, "Nothing Hokey about Hoagies!" and "Save the E.C.A.'s! Buy a hoagie!"

I haven't heard much from Kimberly or Bobby, either. All I know about the car wash is that the school parking lot is *not* available this Saturday, so Bobby's trying to find another time. And Kimberly said everybody's been so busy with exams, nobody's had time to dig up their "white elephants." Oh, well. Maybe next week.

Anyway. Right now the time is . . . ten-hundred hours . . . and I'm waiting for my parents to get back from the grocery store so we can go watch the soccer game which starts at eleven. Both Mom and Dad are real soccer fans. And I figure it this way, E.D. . . . with Dad on the sidelines, the soccer team will make at least *one* hoagie sale today!

Oh—there's the car horn. Gotta jet!

Over and out, E.D.

— *Click!* —

Yahoo! We won the game, E.D.! I think George and Bobby and the other soccer guys must've been letting off steam after exam week because they really tore up the field.

And Dad finally got his hoagie which he enjoyed right down to the last pickle—and he only used thirteen napkins to clean himself up afterwards! But . . . overall I don't think they were selling too hot. There was still a whole box of them left at the end of the game.

— *Click!* —

It's now Monday . . . Day 4,877 . . . Time: sixteen-thirty hundred hours . . . and I'm supervising Rebecca and Matt's homework after school up here in my room. They're not speaking to each other today so at least it's relatively quiet!

It's also Day Thirteen of O.S.B.C. . . . and Kimberly and her cohorts kicked off their three-day White Elephant Sale in the cafeteria today. Kimberly's something else! She really pulled it together over the weekend. I never saw so much junk . . . er, treasures . . . in my life! A lot of kids were looking at all the stuff—everything from old Barbie doll collections to a hamster cage (minus the hamster), baseball cards to comic books, old record albums to scuba masks . . . just hope it results in some big bucks!

As for the car wash . . . I still haven't heard from Bobby—

What's that, Matt? . . . *Another* Code-Buster contest is starting on WWEN today? . . . Well, okay. You can turn my radio on . . . just keep it down so it doesn't bother your sister . . .

Oh, brother, E.D. I thought when the last Code-Buster contest ended last Friday we might have a little peace and quiet around here. Oh, well . . . maybe those word puzzles will help Matt with his spelling—

Riiiiinng.

Disney World . . . Goofy speaking . . .

— *Click!* —

Yes!

That was Bobby, E.D. He finally got permission from Mrs. Long to use the parking lot after school on Wednesday from four to seven for the car wash.

All right! We're rolling now! By Thursday we oughta be able to add up all our proceeds and see how close we've come to our goal. I'd better get that progress chart finished so we can—

Whazzat, Matt? . . . Yes, that's how you spell *fire truck* . . . good job!

— *Click!* —

Same time, same place . . . different day. We had a short schedule today—teachers' workshop or something—so I got home early. I'm going to take advantage of the peace and quiet to catch up in my electronic diary before Matt and Rebecca get here.

It's now Thursday, E.D. . . . Day Sixteen of our

school budget crisis. I called a meeting of the Operation Band Aid committee right after lunch to get the results of our "Save the E.C.A.'s!" fund-raisers. I hung my poster—the one with the lo-o-ong thermometer going all the way from zero to ten thousand bucks—in the hallway, scrounged up a card table and four chairs from the teachers' lounge, and we were ready for roll call.

"Kimberly?" I said. "We're ready for your report."

Kimberly was positively beaming. "The famous White Elephant Sale reports—ta-da!—a solid gain of $352."

"Excellent!" I said, tapping in $352 on my calculator. "A pachyderm-sized response. . . ."

At that moment, a herd of elephants charged out of my imagination and into the hallway of Hampton Falls Junior High, breaking down the doors, throwing up their trunks and trumpeting loudly, announcing the wildly successful White Elephant Sale . . .

I blinked and the hallway returned to its normal lunchtime chaos of kids banging lockers, pushing each other around, and in general getting away with jungle behavior.

But no elephants.

I turned to the guys. "Bobby?"

Bobby hung one arm over the back of his chair and cleared his throat. "Well . . ." he said, "the car wash made ninety-three dollars—"

"Pretty good!" George interrupted.

". . . but we coulda made more," Bobby continued, "if it wasn't for Mrs. King's sunroof."

"Sunroof?" I said. "Oh, no . . . what happened?"

Bobby squirmed. "Well . . . let's just say she got a special outside *and* inside wash."

I could hardly believe my ears. "You *flooded* her car?" . . .

Suddenly all I could hear was the roar of ocean waves crashing on the rocks along the seacoast . . . and as the waves drained back into the sea, I saw a car—not just any car, but Mrs. King's brand-new Mercedes with its fancy sunroof wide open—sitting all by itself out there on the

rocks, washed again and again by the waves out-
side . . . filling up with water inside . . .

Bobby's voice brought me back to the hallway.
"Uh-huh," he admitted. "Baaaad for business."

"Oh, boy . . ." I said, shaking my head. I turned
hopefully to George. "What about you?"

George jerked his thumb in the direction of a
box of hoagies sitting on the floor. "Soccer Team
Hoagie Sale came out to . . . uh, forty-three dollars
after expenses."

"Forty-three?" I asked. "That's it?"

George grimaced. "They haven't been selling so
well."

"A slight understatement," Bobby muttered.

I took a deep breath. "Well . . . that brings our
grand total to . . ." I tapped the rest of the numbers
into my calculator. ". . . an astonishingly bad $488."

I turned to the progress chart on the wall, and
colored in the space just below the five-hundred
dollar mark with a red marker. "We're somewhat
short of our goal, guys," I said . . . not that it wasn't
obvious.

The four of us just stared at the little red mark at
the bottom of the progress chart.

Finally Kimberly threw up her hands. "Drea, we
might as well face it," she said. "It's impossible for
us to raise all the money we need."

I whirled on her. "You guys aren't ready to give

up are you? Just because we've had a little set-back?"

Kimberly, George, and Bobby all looked at each other, then back at me.

"Yeah!" they chorused.

I glared at each one of my so-called buddies in turn. "Let me get this straight. You're just going to sit back and let them take away all of our E.C.A.'s?" I jabbed my finger at Bobby. "No more away soccer games!" Then to Kimberly: "No more drama club productions!" Finally I leaned close to George and reminded him, "No more buses for field trips to the Annual Science Fair—"

Suddenly, out of the blue, I heard another voice cut in.

"—And no more stupid little schemes."

Just what I needed, E.D. . . . Arlene Blake breathing down my neck. And right behind her was Marcy Mannington.

I turned and faced my adversary. As usual, everything about Arlene matched . . . from her white T-neck, yellow-and-white striped sweater, and white skirt, right down to her white tights and yellow canvas purse on a long strap over her shoulder "just so."

"Drea," Arlene continued, in that disdainful voice of hers, "beam back to earth. Face it . . . you've failed."

"Big time!" added Marcy.

I searched Marcy's face for that . . . that *person* I thought I saw who had wanted to sign up for girls' volleyball . . . but she was gone. In her place was Arlene's shadow.

"So, Arlene," I said calmly, "as class president, what would you suggest we do about the E.C.A. cuts?"

Arlene gave a little shrug. "Nothing."

"Zippo . . ." piped up Marcy. "Zilch . . . zero . . . nada . . ."

Marcy was getting on my *nerves*, E.D., but I tried to ignore her.

Arlene looked around at the rest of the committee. "We're seventh graders, after all," she said, talking to us as if we were in kindergarten. "We can't be expected to make that kind of money."

"Wampum . . . greenbacks . . . bucks . . ." Marcy echoed.

I glared at Marcy. "We *know* what money is, Marcy." I turned back to Arlene. "So . . . our class president is just going to sit back and do nothing while the highlights of our educational experience are taken away?"

Arlene permitted herself a little smile as she looked at our "progress" chart.

"Drea," she said, "for the past two weeks, you and your little committee have tried everything . . . and you're still, like, *thousands* short . . ."

"Under . . . shy . . ." said the echo—but this time

it was Arlene who glared at Marcy. ". . . uh, short," Marcy finished weakly.

Arlene looked me up and down, and I knew she was snickering inside at the way I dress—which today was my wide, black-and-white checked pants, big shirt, black vest, and yellow bow tie—an outfit I especially like, E.D.

"Give it up, Drea," she said, "or become the poster child for National Chumps Week. Come on, Marcy . . . let's leave before some of this loser dust rubs off on us."

And with that, Arlene pushed my chair out of her way, and sailed regally down the hall with The Shadow in her wake—

Oh, wait a minute, E.D. . . . I hear the kids coming up the stairs . . . oh, no—they're fighting again!

— *Click!* —

I'm back, but it took a few minutes to settle them down. Matt came stomping in, looking like he'd just eaten a turnip. Rebecca was hot on his heels, and they were going at it like cats and dogs.

"How do you spell *astronaut*?" she demanded.

"Forget it, Rebecca," Matt pouted.

"Matt," she insisted, "Mom told me to help you with your spelling."

"I don't need help," he said.

Rebecca folded her arms and peered at Matt

through her wire rims. "You just don't know how to spell *astronaut*," she said scornfully.

"Do to," Matt shot back.

"Do not."

"Do!"

"Not!"

"Whoa, whoa, whoa!" I broke in. "What's the deal?"

Rebecca rolled her eyes heavenward. "Matt is still doing really badly in spelling at school, and Mom wants me to help him, but he's too . . ." She turned and made a face at Matt. ". . . S-T-U-B-B-O-R-N."

Matt looked like he was going to cry. "See, Drea?" he said. "She just spells all the hard words, then treats me like I'm dumb."

Anyway. I finally got them both working on their homework—at separate places in the room. Matt asked if he could turn the radio on low so he could hear the next Code-Buster clue when it comes on WWEN. I said okay . . . what harm can it do?

So now . . . where was I? Better rewind this and see where I left off.

— *Click!* —

Oh, yeah. Arlene and Marcy had just managed to thoroughly *SMASH* our fund-raising ideas like they were squashing bugs.

"Can you believe what she said?" I fumed when

they were gone.

Kimberly, George, and Bobby looked uncomfortable. Finally George said, "Drea . . . honestly . . . Arlene's right. Unless we can think of a better way to raise the rest of the ten thousand dollars . . . we can just kiss the E.C.A.'s good-bye."

Well, E.D., that was hard to hear—from George, of all people. But . . . I have to admit our fund-raising ideas so far have fallen a little short—okay, okay, a *lot* short—but I, for one, am not ready to give up without a fight. But I wish I could come up with a new idea soon . . . I can hardly concentrate on my homework or *anything*! All I can think about is how to make big bucks fast—

Wait . . . wait! . . . Matt! Turn up that radio!

— *Click!* —

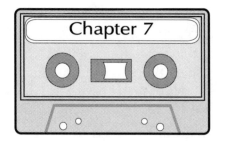

Chapter 7

Clueless in Hampton Falls

I can't believe it, E.D.! The answer to getting our extracurricular activities back has been under my nose the whole time, and I didn't see it!

Matt had my radio on . . . ya know, listening for WWEN's Code-Buster clues . . . and the deejay was hyping: "You're listening to WWEN . . . Power Ten-Forty! Hey, is anybody out there ready to play . . ." —sudden deep voice— ". . . *CODE-BUSTER*? Remember, you're playing for . . . *TEN THOUSAND DOLLARS* . . ."

And it hit me in a *SMASH*! If I could win the Code-Buster contest, we could get all our E.C.A.'s back with the prize money!

The deejay was saying, "If you can make any

cents out of these clues, call me! The clues so far are . . ."

I grabbed a pad of paper while the deejay rattled off, ". . . FIRE TRUCK . . . PLANET . . . GUITAR . . . ." Then there was a drum roll and the deejay said mysteriously: "And today's clue is . . . SAW."

I could tell Matt wanted to ask me why I was writing down the Code-Buster clues . . . but he was still mad at Rebecca and didn't want to ruin the pout he was in. I saw him write down the last clue—at least SAW is a word he can spell all by himself.

What a weird combination of words! I lay back on my bed, stared at the slanted ceiling of my attic bedroom, and let my imagination play around with the words . . .

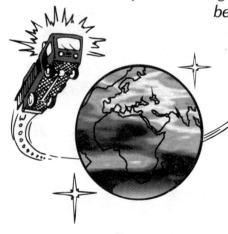

As I stared at my overhead light, it suddenly began to grow larger and larger, spinning around like a PLANET in the solar system. A satellite appeared over the horizon, with little red

*lights winking . . . no, it wasn't a satellite after all,
but a FIRE TRUCK soaring around the planet, siren
wailing, lights flashing! . . . As it came around the
curve of the planet, the fire truck screeched to a
stop right on the equator . . . a fireman jumped out
with a big SAW, and proceeded to cut the planet in
half . . . when it fell open, the two halves formed
the sound board of a GUITAR . . .*

I shook my head to clear my brain and thought,
Nah, I don't think so.

But . . . I've been staring at the four clues for the
last five minutes, E.D., and at this point they don't
make any more sense to me than they do to Matt!
Sigh. I know trying to win a radio contest isn't an
sure-fire idea for getting our E.C.A.'s back, but it
equals about . . . oh, five thousand hours of baby-
sitting, so I guess I'll give it a whirl—

Riiiinng.

Just a sec, E.D. . . . gotta get the phone . . .

Never-Neverland . . . this is Wendy . . .

— Click! —

Well, that was a *long* second. First the phone . . .
then I had to help Rebecca with a homework
problem.

But back to the phone call. It was Kimberly,
gushing like Old Faithful.

"Drea, I've got a big, big, *big* idea," she said.

"Me, too!" I cut in, waving my pad of paper with the four clues written on it. "I'm going to win the Code-Buster contest on WWEN!"

There was a slight pause on the other end of the line.

"Okaaay . . ." Kimberly said doubtfully, "that's kinda far out, too. But . . . just listen to my idea. Who's the richest dudette at school?"

"Richest?" I frowned. "I dunno."

"I'll give you a hint," Kimberly gushed on. "Her grandfather owns a Fortune 500 company . . ."

As if I knew the job descriptions and bank accounts of all the relatives of the kids at school.

". . . he has his own charity . . . ," Kimberly hinted.

Blank. Zero. Nothing.

Kimberly pushed on with her guessing game. ". . . as in donates money? . . . to worthy causes?"

I rolled my eyes. "I hope this isn't a sign of how I'm gonna do on guessing the Code-Buster clues," I groaned.

"Okay, last hint," Kimberly said. "Her grandfather donated Falls Park, *and* he's coming to Hampton Falls *this weekend* to get an award!"

"I give up!" I said, slightly exasperated. How in the world was I supposed to know who donated Falls Park? It's been there since before I was born.

"Arlene Blake!" Kimberly's voice was triumphant.

"*Our* Arlene Blake?" I repeated . . . not sure I wanted to hear the rest of Kimberly's big idea.

"Yes!" Kimberly was so excited, I had to hold the telephone away from my ear. "Which means . . . in one phone call, Arlene could replace the entire amount that's been dropped from the E.C.A. budget, if . . ."

I didn't like the sound of this.

"If what?" I asked suspiciously.

"If *you* can convince her to make the call," Kimberly said quickly.

My response was swift and strong. "*What?! Me?! Why?!*"

"It's brilliant, Drea . . . look, you call her and you go, 'Arlene, all my ideas for getting our E.C.A.'s back are totally pea-brained.' And then you say, 'The only way I could look like any more of a loser is if *you* talked your grandfather into giving us the dough.' "

"You have *got* to be kidding me," I said dryly.

"Drea . . . you know she'd do it. I mean . . . it'll work!"

"But," I protested, wondering why Kimberly was overlooking the obvious, "I'll look totally lame, and Arlene will look like a hero to the whole school."

"Exactly!" Kimberly crowed. "That's what makes 'Operation Beg and Grovel' so brilliant! Arlene won't be able to resist making an absolute fool of you!"

Can you believe it, E.D.? Beg and grovel indeed! Sometimes I wonder . . . with a best friend like Kimberly, who needs—

Whoa! What's this? . . . Who . . .?

— *Click!* —

Well, E.D., it's times like that that I wish you were a *video* diary instead of an *audio* diary.

All of a sudden my bedroom door burst open, and this . . . this weird person came marching pompously into my attic room . . . dressed like somebody from the eighteenth century! I mean, starting with the buckle shoes, white tights, britches cut off at the knee, a blue brocade waistcoat with pockets big enough to stick New Jersey into, with some kinda lacy stuff sticking out at the cuffs and neck . . . and to top it all off, a white, powdered wig!

My eyes popped out—*zingo!*—and I did a doubletake before I dared take a guess. "Uh . . . Da—ad?"

It was Dad all right, grinning under that powdered wig. "I'm just getting ready for my 'Sixty Minuets with Wolfie Mozart' concert," he said in a thick brogue, which I *think* was supposed to be an Austrian accent. "This is my idea for how to publicize the Mozart concert! You know . . . walking around the college campus in costume . . . making people curious . . . serving as a reminder to come listen to Wolfie Mozart and his brilliant music."

"Nice idea, Dad," I said. "It might even work."

He turned around slowly so Rebecca and Matt, at their separate desks doing homework, could get the full effect of his costume. "Whatcha think, kids?"

Rebecca glanced up and shrugged. "Looks fine, Mr. Thomas," she said, then turned back to her schoolwork.

Matt was equally unimpressed. "Yeah . . . nice shoes," he murmured, and went back to copying his letters.

My dad was flabbergasted. He leaned close to me and whispered, "Drea, what's up with those two? This outfit should get a beeg laugh!"

I raised my eyes to the ceiling at his attempt at a accent. "Sorry, Dad," I said. "They're in the middle of an argument . . ." —I raised my voice so both kids could hear— ". . . *and they'd hate to say anything nice to ruin it.*"

Poor Dad was desperate for a reaction. "But, Drea . . . I'm going for Baroque here . . . heh, heh."

I shook my head. "V.B.J."

Dad looked puzzled. "V.B.J?"

"Very Bad Joke," I explained. I mean, adults need to realize there's a limit on how funny they think they are.

"Oh . . . I see," he said. He shrugged, then jerked his thumb toward Matt and Rebecca. "Well, should we tell them that their M-O-M is H-E-R-E?"

Matt's spelling must be getting better, because his reaction was explosive. Stuffing his papers into his book bag, he ran toward the stairs. "I'm gonna tell M-O-M what you did!" he yelled back at Rebecca. " 'Bye, Drea! . . . *Mom!*"

Rebecca was hot on his heels. "Not if I get there F-I-R-S-T! . . . 'Bye, Drea! . . . Mom! Don't listen to Matt!"

Dad grinned, looking sorta boyish and cute under that silly, powdered white wig, like a kid playing dress up. "Well. That certainly perked them right up . . ."

Then we must have had the same thought at the same instant, because we both yelled after them, "No running on the S-T-E-P-S!"

After Dad left, I worked some more on the Code-Buster contest. I'm absolutely sure I can break this code . . . I'm just not sure it will happen in this millennium! It's certainly got to be easier than "begging and groveling" at Arlene's feet. But between thinking so hard about Operation Band Aid and how to raise money to get our E.C.A.'s back, and trying to figure out how to get Rebecca and Matt to stop arguing about everything, my brain feels fried—

Hey, I hear my fans calling . . . okay, so it's just Mom calling me to set the table. But that means dinner must be almost ready . . . and I'm famished!

Over and out, E.D.

— *Click!* —

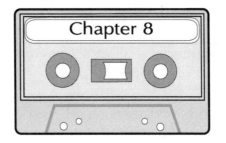

It's a Jungle in Here!

Dear E.D. . . . it's Friday, Day 4,881 in the Secret Adventures of yours truly . . . and I'm checking in as I ride my bike home from school.

It's also Day Seventeen of O.S.B.C. . . . but on my way to school this morning I was all revved up to solve this Code-Buster thing, and I was feeling pretty good when I walked into school.

Matt said radio station WWEN has been giving a new clue every day, so I was using the earphones to my Walkman as I walked down the hall toward my locker. And sure enough the Code-Buster theme music came up, and the deejay yelled into my ears, "Okaaaaay, Code-Busters! Get ready for today's clue . . . BANANA."

That's it, E.D. . . . "banana." The other four clues are strange enough. But, I mean . . . what kind of clue is "banana"?

I was muttering, "Banana? . . . banana?" as I opened my locker, trying to fit it together with the other clues, when suddenly my locker door slammed shut, and there stood the person I least wanted to see right then.

Arlene Blake.

She gave my clothes a scornful glance, obviously contrasting my red checked pants, blue vest, and big shirt with her "preppy" white T-neck, navy blazer, and short skirt. Oh, yes, I almost forgot her fancy "A" initial pin.

"*Excuse me,* Drea," she said. "I just heard your latest scheme to raise thousands of dollars is to win a radio contest." She rolled her eyes and laughed. "It's . . . so *you*! Who else would come up with such a crazy, hopeless idea? I mean . . . what's the likelihood of winning? A zillion to one?" By this time her voice was dripping with sarcasm. "*Great* plan!" With that, Arlene shouldered me aside and strutted over to her own locker.

Personally, E.D., I'm getting *extremely* tired of being insulted by Arlene . . .

Standing there in the school hallway, I felt like a mini-volcano inside, with the lava starting to boil somewhere down in my mid-section. Dangerous

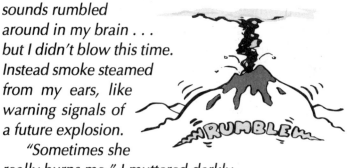

sounds rumbled around in my brain . . . but I didn't blow this time. Instead smoke steamed from my ears, like warning signals of a future explosion.

"Sometimes she really burns me," I muttered darkly . . .

But my little encounter with Arlene this morning helped resolve one thing for me, E.D. There's *no way* I could ever beg Arlene Blake to do something . . . even to save the E.C.A.'s! Which means I've gotta win the WWEN contest, defin-a-mundo—

Oh, no. There's Rebecca and Matt on their way to my house . . . and I can hear them arguing from here! Looks like I've got another problemo to solve first.

— Click! —

Still Friday, Day 4,881 . . . Time: almost eighteen-hundred hours . . . and I'm cleaning up a big mess from—

Wait. I better back up and start where I left off, when Matt and Rebecca arrived at my house after school. Matt was in his normal "uniform" of pullover shirt, jeans, and baseball cap, but Rebecca had a new hair style—a long braid down her back—and an outfit of blue-flowered stretch pants and top had replaced her normal skirt and sweater. But that was the only thing that was different. She was *still* on Matt's case about his spelling . . .

"Spell *eclipse*," she challenged, as they stormed into my bedroom.

"C'mon, Rebecca," he complained. "No way that's a first grade word . . . my teacher couldn't even spell that!"

Rebecca folded her arms. "*I* knew these words when I was your age," she said loftily, looking down her nose at Matt through her wire-rimmed glasses.

"No way!" Matt challenged.

"Yes way!" she insisted.

"No!"

"Yes!"

Well, by that time, E.D., I had had it with those two! This competition thing had to stop . . . and the only thing I could think of that might work was a little safari into my imagination. I stared at the door going off from my room into the unfinished part of the attic and got an idea . . .

A wild trumpeting sound seemed to shake the whole house, followed by a noisy racket of screeching and squawking . . .

Matt and Rebecca both jumped.

"What was that?!" Matt said, his eyes wide.

I looked around innocently. "What was what?"

Both kids pointed anxiously at my attic door. So I motioned to them and we crept closer, putting our ears to the door . . .

This time we heard a deep, throaty roar behind the door, setting off a new hubbub of screeching and squawking . . .

Matt tugged on my shirt. "Drea," he whispered suspiciously. "What's going on?"

I grinned slyly. "S-E-C-R-E-T . . ." I spelled slowly, ". . . A-D-V-E-N-T-U-R-E."

Puzzled, Matt turned and looked at Rebecca. "See . . . see-creet . . . ?" he mumbled, trying to sound it out.

Rebecca started to grin as she silently mouthed the words. I was reaching for the doorknob when Matt figured it out and whirled back to me. "A Secret Adventure! . . ."

". . . Whoaaaaaaa!" he yelped, as I pulled both kids into the attic and closed the door behind us.

But I could hardly see a thing! The light was very dim, and all around us were thick, green plants . . . some with big broad leaves, others with tall, skinny spikes, all tangled up with vines and bushes and long tendrils of moss dripping from eucalyptus trees.

Somewhere in the brush I heard Matt's voice saying breathlessly, "Where are we?"

Then Rebecca's voice: "You mean, WHAT are we?"

I looked this way and that, but I couldn't see them anywhere. So I pushed a big, broad palm leaf out of my face . . . and stepped into a little clearing. Long shafts of sunlight streamed down through the canopy of palm leaves overhead, brightening the dark jungle on either side. The clearing was empty . . . but just then the bushes around me started to rustle and shake. A moment later a small, brown monkey with a long, skinny tail and a base- ball cap rolled out of the brush and landed with a SPLAT! on the mossy, jungle floor.

"Hi, Matt!" I greeted the monkey. "Where's—"

"Right here," said Rebecca . . . and sure enough, a baby elephant with wire-rimmed glasses balanced on her long trunk tumbled out of the forest.

"Ha-ha-ha-heh-heh," giggled Matt the monkey, pointing a brown finger in her direction. "Look, Drea . . . Rebecca's an elephant! Heh-heh-ha-ha . . ."

Rebecca flapped her wide, elephant ears in a huff. "Well, YOU'RE a monkey—"

"AHEM!" I interrupted. Both the little elephant and the monkey looked up at me. And I mean UP.

"Wow!" Matt said, bouncing excitedly around the little clearing on his long arms. "Drea's a . . . a giraffe!"

Ah-ha, I thought. So that's why they looked so far away down there! I bent my long neck down and around and examined my yellow and brown  spots first from one side, then the other. Then I straightened up again and looked around.

"Hey, being a giraffe is great," I said. "I can see high, I can see low, I can see—wait! What's that?"

Along the edge of the clearing was a strange pile of leaves and moss that looked kinda funny. I walked over to it—it only took two or three steps with my long giraffe legs—and bent my head down to look at it.

"Rebecca . . . Matt . . . come see this," I called. "But be very careful . . . this is an animal trap."

Matt bounced over, a bundle of monkey energy, with Rebecca lumbering not far behind on her four, short, gray legs. "Look." I motioned with my long neck. "See that rope leading out of the pile of leaves and running along the ground to that tree over there?"

"Uh-huh," said Rebecca . . . then suddenly her trunk began twitching. "Ah . . . ah . . . ah-choo! Ah-choo!" she sneezed, blasting Matt the monkey head over heels into the bushes. "Whew . . . there must be a cat around here," she said.

Matt untangled himself from a long vine. "Oh, great," he muttered, "even as an elephant, she's got allergies—"

Just then an ear-splitting scream pierced the jungle.

"Eiee . . . eiee!" squeaked Matt, jumping five feet off the ground and throwing his arms around my neck. I whirled and faced the direction that awful sound came from. Rebecca tried to hide her stout, little elephant body between my long legs; she was trembling all over.

But now there was only silence.

Then . . . a twig snapped in the underbrush . . .

then another.

"Shhh . . . do you guys hear that?" I whispered.

"Gulp . . . uh-huh," Matt breathed.

"Uh-huh," said Rebecca, ". . . oh . . . ah . . . cat . . . AHHH . . ."

In a split second, Matt leaped off my neck and tried to wrap his long tail around the elephant's trunk. "Rebecca, no—!" he cried.

But it was too late. ". . . CHOO!" sneezed Rebecca.

Another snarl—closer this time—answered.

"Drea!" screamed Rebecca. "It IS a cat—a BIG cat."

"Y-y-you mean . . . ?" stuttered the little monkey.

"YES!" I shouted. "A panther! Let's get outta here!"

We all started to run . . . and crashed right into each other.

"This way!" yelled Rebecca.

"No, this way!" yelled Matt, grabbing a vine and starting to swing into the trees.

As the monkey swung past the baby elephant, Rebecca grabbed him with her trunk, pulled him right up to her eyeballs, and said, "Some of us can't go up trees, dork."

"Oh," said Matt.

But a loud snarl in the bushes sent the little monkey scurrying up the closest tree anyway. "I'll be right back!" he yelled over his shoulder.

I knew that panther was somewhere close by, crouching for an attack. Rebecca begged me to run, but I couldn't just leave Matt up in the tree. I craned my long neck, trying to see what was happening up there. Then I realized what he was doing . . . he was picking coconuts and throwing them at the panther as fast as he could!

"Bull's eye!" laughed Matt, throwing and chattering away from the top of the palm tree. "Bull's eye again—right on the noggin! . . . Hey, guys!" Matt was pointing excitedly. "I see a cave!"

I glanced anxiously toward the bushes, which were suddenly quiet, then back up at Matt. "Where?" I yelled.

"I'll show ya!" he said, shimmying back down the tree trunk. He came down that trunk so fast, it looked like the tree trunk had been greased. To

84

break his speed, Matt grabbed a vine-looking thing wrapped around the tree.

"Hissssssssssss," said The Thing, unwrapping itself from the tree trunk and staring the little monkey in the eye.

"Whoaaa," gulped Matt. "Sorry about that, Mr. Snake."

The little monkey let go and dropped the last few feet to the ground.

"C'mon, guys," he said to me and Rebecca, "the cave's right through . . . uh . . . there."

"There" was a bamboo forest growing so close together it looked like a wall.

"What??" I protested. "I can't go through there!" A giraffe might be skinny, but not THAT skinny.

Behind us we heard the panther snarl again . . . and this time he sounded really angry.

"Well, I can!" said Rebecca, rearing back on her hind legs. "Follow me!" The baby elephant charged into the forest, butting the bamboo "wall" full force with her broad head. The bamboo cracked and fell right and left as she trampled a path into the jungle.

"Hooray for Rebecca!" I yelled. "C'mon, Matt!"

Matt leaped on my back, wrapping his long monkey arms around my neck, and we galloped after the elephant, who was churning like a Hot Wheels Racer through the jungle. I could hear snarling and crashing behind me.

"Faster, Drea, faster!" squeaked Matt, hanging on for dear life.

Just ahead I saw Rebecca break out of the dense jungle growth. "The cave must be right up ahead!" I told Matt, who was holding so tightly to my neck I could hardly breathe. Then the little elephant screeched to a stop so suddenly, I piled right into her.

"Ooof!"

"Ugh!"

"Ouch!"

After we all untangled ourselves, we quickly looked around. There was a rock cliff right in front of us, and boulders piled everywhere. But where was the cave?

"Uh-oh," I heard Matt say. "Uh . . . there it is."

There was a cave all right . . . but with so many boulders, bushes, and vines tangled all around the opening that all three of us would never get in.

Just then we heard a large thud and a loud snarl. Whipping around, my heart almost stopped.

We were face to face with the largest black panther I had ever seen in my life, muscles rippling under glossy, black fur, with sharp teeth and narrow, glittering eyes.

And this panther wasn't behind bars in a zoo, either.

So I did what any self-respecting giraffe would do when confronted by a sleek, snarling jungle cat.

"Aiiiiieeeee!" I screamed.

"Aiiiiieeeee!" screamed the baby elephant and the monkey.

"Aiiiiieeeeeeeeeeeeeeeeeeeeeeeeeeeeeeeeee!"

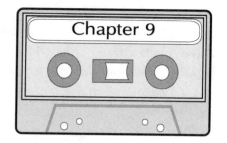

Booby Trapped!

We immediately scattered. Out of the corner of my eye I saw the panther go after Matt, but the little monkey quickly grabbed a vine and pulled himself, hand over hand, out of reach.

I took the opportunity to duck behind a tall palm tree, making myself as skinny as I could. But inside my giraffe body, my heart was thumping wildly. Was my tail showing? Would the panther find me? And . . . where was Rebecca the elephant?

I listened, but could hear nothing. What was happening? Slowly I poked my nose around the tree trunk and peeked . . . and there was the panther looking right in my direction! Quickly I pulled my nose back behind the tree, but not before I saw the panther take a great leap toward my tree!

Oh, no! I thought. He's gonna find me . . .

Just then I saw the panther slide into view . . . but he was looking behind other trees and hadn't seen me yet. I knew it was just a question of time. What should I do? Should I run? Should I stay still and hope he didn't see me? Should I—

Suddenly I heard a loud, "AHHH . . . CHOO!"

It was Rebecca!

The panther's head swung away from me in the direction of the sneeze. I poked my head around the tree to see what was happening. Rebecca was still standing near the cave opening! Why hadn't the little elephant run away?

Rebecca saw the panther, too. "Oh, no-o-o . . . I'm a goner!" she moaned.

With a wicked snarl, the panther bounded back into the rocky clearing, licked his chops—yum! yum!—and began to circle his prey.

Rebecca just stood still, like a statue. "He-elp," she called weakly.

Well! I couldn't just stand behind a tree and do nothing! I was just about to leap out when I heard a loud, warbling yell come whizzing right past my ear.

"Ah-ee-ah-ee-ah-ee-ah-ee-ah-ee-ahhhhhhhhhh!!"

A brown blur swung out of the trees on a long vine, yelling just like Tarzan, the jungle ape-man. As the vine swung into the clearing, the brown, furry ball leaped off the vine and onto the back of the panther.

It was Matt the monkey!

"Run, Rebecca!" yelled Matt, as the panther twisted and bucked, trying to get the monkey off his back.

"I can't!" cried Rebecca the elephant. "My foot's stuck! . . . Ah . . . ahhh . . . choo! Ah-choo!"

Sure enough. Between sneezes, the little elephant was trying to pull her foot up, but it was wedged tightly between two heavy rocks. I could see her trembling all over. We had to do something fast, or Rebecca was a goner for sure!

"We gotta do something!" Matt yelled, trying to stay out of reach of those slashing fangs. "I can't be the monkey on this guy's back forever!"

My mind raced. Then I remembered something. If only we could . . .

We only had one chance. Boldly I galloped into the clearing. "Ride 'em, cowboy!" I hollered, getting the panther's attention . . . then I took off running back through the jungle along the "trail" Rebecca had mashed down with her elephant feet.

Forgetting the monkey on his back, the panther took off after me. I could hear him snarling and snapping at my hooves as I galloped through the bamboo, bushes, and vines as fast as my long, giraffe legs would take me.

"Whoaaaaaaaaaa . . . !" yelped Matt behind me. I risked a look, and saw the little monkey clutching the panther's neck fur, trying not to fall off.

The other clearing was just up ahead. But if my trick was going to work, Matt had to get off the panther's back!

"Jump, Matt, jump!" I cried, as I sped into the clearing and swerved quickly around the little pile of moss and leaves. Then I skidded to a stop and whirled around. Either my trick was going to work . . . or Matt and I were goners.

Then the panther's paws landed on the little pile of moss and leaves—and with a loud, "WHOOSH!" the panther was swept up into the air in a big, strong net.

"Hooray!" I cried. My trick had worked! The panther was caught in the animal trap that had

almost caught us earlier!

But . . . where was Matt? Oh, no! Was he caught in the net, too?

But just then I heard a friendly, "Hisssssssssssss."

 There, hanging down out of the trees, just inches from the net, was Mr. Snake. And dangling by his long, monkey arms from Mr. Snake's curved body was . . . Matt.

The little monkey dropped to the ground. "Whew!" he said, looking up at the slithering reptile. "That was close! Thanks a lot, Mr. Snake."

"Sssssssssssssssssure thing," hissed the snake sleepily. "Gotta cooperate if you're gonna sssssssssssssurvive in the jungle." With that, the snake looped himself back up into the tree, looking just like another fat vine.

Inside the net, the panther—who had been blinking in bewilderment—was starting to struggle and snarl.

"C'mon, Matt, let's get out of here," I said, heading back toward the cave and Rebecca.

The poor little elephant's foot was still wedged tightly between the rocks.

"What happened!?" she demanded, relieved to see us come back. "I thought for sure you guys were goners!"

"We'll tell you," I said, "but first . . . we gotta get you outta here."

Matt grabbed hold of one rock with his monkey hands and I placed both my giraffe front hooves against the other.

"Pull!" grunted Matt.

"Push!" I grunted.

"Wait!" said Rebecca. "I have to . . . to . . . ah . . . ahhhhhh . . ."

". . . CHOO!" sneezed Rebecca as she blinked her watery eyes and looked around. The three of us were sitting on some old suitcases in the unfinished attic, surrounded by cardboard boxes, stacks of magazines, and old furniture.

"Boy . . . it sure is dusty in here," she sniffled.

Matt looked suspiciously around the attic, to be sure the boxes and furniture were just that . . . boxes and furniture.

"Whew!" he said. "That was close."

"Yeah," Rebecca nodded solemnly. "Thanks, guys . . . if it hadn't been for you, I'd be cat food."

Matt nodded, too. "Yeah . . . if we hadn't worked together, none of us would have made it!"

Matt and Rebecca looked at each other as if they were thinking hard.

"I'm sorry—" they started to say together.

"—for picking on you about your spelling," Rebecca finished.

"Me, too," said Matt. "I mean . . . I'm sorry for being so stubborn that I wouldn't let you help me."

I was just about to open my mouth when both kids looked at me.

"Sorry to you, too, Drea," Rebecca sighed. "Guess we've made life kinda hard for you the last couple of weeks."

Now *there* was an understatement, E.D.

Matt shrugged. "Yeah . . . what she said."

I couldn't help it, E.D. . . . they looked so remorseful I almost wanted to laugh. But instead I just held out my arms and gave them both a giant hug.

We climbed back out of the attic into my room, and after brushing the dust and cobwebs off our clothes, decided to forget homework—it's Friday, after all!—and go make jack-o'-lanterns out of those pumpkins Grandpa brought a couple weeks ago.

Funny thing . . . Matt's jack-o'-lantern looked just like a monkey!

Mrs. Long came and picked up the kids about half an hour ago, and now I'm trying to clean up all the pumpkin mess before Mom and Dad get home. But . . . something about that Secret Adventure is nagging at me, E.D. I think that whole "cooperation" thing has to do with something bigger than just the petty quarrels Matt and Rebecca get themselves into . . .

Over and out for now.

— *Click!* —

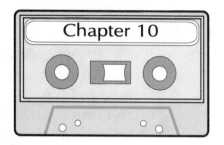

Humble Pie Has No Calories

Checking in, E.D. . . . it's Monday morning . . . Day 4,884 . . . Time: oh-seven-hundred hours . . . and I'm in the kitchen fortifying myself with a good breakfast before I take up Operation Band Aid again.

Ya see, E.D., all weekend I've been thinkin' about that little Secret Adventure I took with Rebecca and Matt. I was trying to get them to think about cooperation being more important than who's right and who's wrong . . . it's putting aside your differences and working together to make something good happen. But—

Just a minute, E.D. . . . I want to check my toast . . .

As I reach for my slice of toast in our antique toaster, a red STOP sign also pops up from the second slot.

"Hold it, Drea," says Mr. Toaster, twitching his big nose and frowning at me. "Isn't this your third piece of toast this morning? What's going on? Usually you're a one-slice-and-I'm-outta-here kind of person!"

"Oh . . . hi, Toaster," I say meekly. "I was just telling my electronic diary that I need an extra big breakfast this morning. Ya see . . . I've decided the only way to save the E.C.A.'s at school is for us to lay aside our differences and work together, but . . . it's gonna take some courage on my part."

"Courage, eh?" says the toaster. "Since when does courage need calories? Once ya decide what ya gotta do, ya just gotta do it! Take me, for example. Why, when I was a brand-new toaster, still wet behind the handles, I—"

"That's okay, Toaster," I say, grinning. "I get your point. And you're right . . . I better forget the third piece of toast and jet outta here."

"That's the spirit! Go for it, Drea!" cheers the toaster as he shoots that piece of toast so far out of its slot that it lands on the floor . . .

Guess I'll forget that third piece of toast, E.D. After all, courage doesn't run on calories. It takes decision...backbone...chutzpah...moxie...grit...

Hmmm. Maybe a few extra calories wouldn't hurt, either. Where'd that toast land?

— *Click!* —

Back again, E.D. . . . same day . . . time: nineteen-hundred hours (otherwise known as seven o'clock and time to do my homework) . . . place: my bedroom . . .

But first, an update on the Humiliation of My Life.

Even with a third piece of toast, I was able to leave early for school to pursue my radical, new approach to saving the E.C.A.'s. I'd decided Kimberly was right: Arlene couldn't resist seeing me "beg and grovel."

Sure enough, there was my prey—I mean, the person I was looking for—walking to school dressed in an expensive, dark green, wool blazer and short, flowered skirt.

"Hey, Arlene!" I called out, sending my Western Flier hurtling toward my target. "Can I talk with you a sec?"

Did she slow down? Look my way? No. Frankly, Arlene just walked faster. But . . . I was determined, so I skidded to a two-tire landing in front of her so she'd have to stop.

Arlene looked really peeved. "Thomas," she said, trying to get around my bike, "I really don't want to be seen with you in public." She gave my red beret and large silk sunflower pinned at my neck a disgusted look.

"It'll only take a minute," I said in a rush. "I've come up with a great, new way that the entire school will be at your feet . . ."

That got her.

"All right," she said, rolling her eyes impatiently. "Make it fast . . . and this better be good."

"Okay, get this," I said, talking fast. "My plan will, number one, absolutely establish you as *the* most popular girl in school . . ."

A single-engine plane slowly circled Hampton Falls Junior High, pulling a long banner with bright red, three-foot-high letters which read: "ARLENE MOST POPULAR" . . .

I double blinked, trying not to "see" the effects of my imagination, and rushed on.

"Number two," I said, "*I'll* do all the work and

you'll get all the credit, which of course will make me look pretty stupid . . ."

The small plane was joined by another single-engine plane, this one pulling a long banner with bright blue, three-foot-high letters which read: "DREA LOOKS STUPID" . . .

I gulped and rushed on. "And number three, you will become the school hero, because you alone will save the E.C.A.'s . . .!"

A third plane joined the other two to the cheers of all 547 Hampton Falls Junior High students as they saw the third banner rippling in the sky, sporting bright green, three-foot-high letters which read: "ARLENE SCHOOL HERO" . . ."

Arlene was looking at me suspiciously. "Okay, okay . . . so what's the catch?"

"Well," I said, taking a big breath, "you convince your grandfather to donate ten thousand dollars to our school."

Arlene's eyebrows went up. "And what's your chance of raising the dinero without my help?" she asked.

Let me tell you, E.D., humble pie was never harder to swallow. "Honestly?" I shook my head. "Not even close."

Arlene pursed her lips. "You know, as much as I loved drama and cheerleading . . ." She paused as a victory sneer flickered across her face. ". . . they've *never* made me feel this good!"

For a second, E.D., I thought she was going to agree! How could she pass up making me look stupid and becoming the school hero in one measly phone call?

But then my hopes came crashing down with a SMASH.

"You are so *pathetic*, Drea Thomas," Arlene said scornfully. "Do you actually think I'm going to help you . . . after all you've done to me? *No way!*"

She pushed my bike handle out of her way and started to leave. Then she turned back. "But don't go away feeling like a total failure," she said sweetly—too sweetly, like honey trapping flies. "After all, to see you groveling so pitifully has really made my day!"

And with that, she walked off to school with her nose in the air.

Talk about *humiliating*, E.D. I wanted to smack Kimberly for getting me into this mess in the first place. Operation Beg and Grovel, indeed! We misjudged Arlene on one crucial point . . . and that is, as much as Arlene Blake would like to be the school hero or make me look stupid, she's *not* willing to lift a finger to help me get something I want . . . even if that means no E.C.A.'s for anybody!—

Oh, hi, Grandpa. Sure, come on in . . . the attic door is right there . . .

— Click! —

That was Grandpa, E.D. He came over to look for some boxes of his stuff he has stored in our attic.

"An old high school buddy of mine is in town visiting his daughter and her family," I heard him saying, his voice muffled by the stacks of boxes and old furniture in there.

"That's nice, Grandpa," I mumbled, wishing I could forget Arlene's withering look as she let me make a fool of myself this morning.

"So . . ." Grandpa said, emerging from the attic door into my bedroom, "I thought I'd have him over, but first I've gotta get my apartment cleaned up."

I managed a grin. "You better hire a cleaning crew," I teased. I mean, face it, E.D., housecleaning isn't one of Grandpa's strong points. He'd rather be outdoors gardening.

"Very funny," Grandpa said, and then he wandered over to where I was slumped at my desk. "I found one of my yearbooks," he continued, holding out a large, dusty book. "He'll get a hoot out of this!"

When I didn't look up, Grandpa bent down and looked into my eyes. "So, why the long face?" he asked.

I shrugged. "Oh, nothing . . . ," I started to say, but I knew better than try to pull that one on Grandpa. "Except that I made an absolute idiot out of myself today," I admitted with a big sigh. "I asked Arlene for help to get our E.C.A.'s back, and she nearly spit on me."

"Ah," said Grandpa. "I see."

I looked up into his face with its warm laugh wrinkles and the concerned look in his eyes.

"You don't happen to have a spare ten grand on you, do ya, Grandpa?" I asked.

He frowned and whipped out his wallet. "Hang on a second . . . hmm. Can you break a twenty thousand dollar bill?"

I grinned. "No," I said, "but that'll cover two years of the E.C.A. budget."

Grandpa stuck his wallet back in his pocket.

"C'mon . . . you got any other ideas?"

I shook my head. "I've run out of ideas," I admitted, "except my zillion-to-one chance of winning the Code-Buster contest on WWEN . . . oh! I almost forgot!"

I jumped up and clicked on my radio by my bed. After all, E.D., I decided that since it's the only idea I've got left, I better catch today's clue!

The WWEN deejay was saying, ". . . and part of our prize package includes two . . . TWO . . . yearly passes to the Hampton Falls Multiplex Cinemas . . ."

Not bad, I thought. If I won, I could save the E.C.A.'s *and* see free movies for a whole year with a friend of my choice . . .

Two movie passes popped up temptingly from the top of my radio and waggled at me, but when I reached out for them, they zipped back inside, giggling, "Heh-heh-heh!" . . .

I was brought back to reality by the deejay announcing ominously, "And now it's time for today's . . . *Code-Buster*."

My list! Where was my list! I frantically fished under my pile of homework on my desk—

"Today's clue is . . . ," the deejay went on.

There! I grabbed my pad of paper while Grandpa handed me his pen.

". . . ARMADILLO," said the radio.

Armadillo? I thought. Did anybody in Hampton Falls know what an armadillo was . . . or care?

As I frowned at the latest clue, I thought I saw a pointed snout poke out of the radio speaker . . . . Then suddenly a strange looking animal in armored skin slithered onto my night table.

"You got a problem with armadillos, kid?" said the creature . . . but before I could say anything, it slid down the leg of the night table, and scurried under my bed . . .

I wrote it down along with the other clues: AR-MADILLO.

The deejay was still working up a sweat. ". . . Be sure to call me here at WWEN—Power Ten-Forty!—if you think you're the . . . *Code-Buster.*"

I clicked off the radio and stared at my list of words. "Grandpa . . . are you any good at breaking codes?" I asked.

Grandpa picked up my list, studied it for a moment, then shook his head. "To break this code, you're gonna need more than just me to help you out!"

Huh! There was that cooperation thing cropping up again!

Grandpa gave me a quick hug and said, "Well, I gotta go clean my apartment before my old high school buddy shows up. Hang in there, Drea!" He gave me a thumbs up and disappeared down the stairs with his old yearbook.

But maybe Grandpa's right, E.D. If breaking this Code-Buster contest is our only chance to get the E.C.A.'s back, what we need now is mega brain power . . . collective mental energy . . . and I know just where to find it!

— *Click!* —

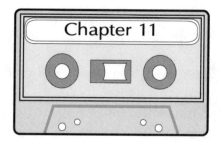

Chapter 11

Operation Win Big

G'morning, E.D.! It's Tuesday morning . . . day twenty-one of O.S.B.C. . . . but I can't talk now. Gotta meet Kimberly at school early to launch phase three of our effort to save the E.C.A.'s . . . which we have renamed Operation Win Big!

Catch ya later!

— *Click!* —

Back again, E.D. . . . just got home from school. Here's an update on Operation Win Big.

Kimberly met me at school early with a stack of papers which listed all the Code-Buster clues so far. Our first victim—er, helper—was George, whom we collared as soon as he came in the front door.

"You wanna help us solve WWEN's Code-Buster contest?" I asked, shoving a sheet of paper into his hand. "Here's the list of clues so far."

"And here are more to hand out in all your classes," Kimberly added, stacking more handouts on top of his other books.

"Uh . . . sure," he said, shrugging. Then we heard him muttering as he went off, "Anything's gotta be easier than selling hoagies . . ."

When we came to the end of the hallway, I veered left and Kimberly turned right, passing out sheets to every kid we saw. Later Kimberly told me she passed Arlene Blake and her shadow—Marcy Mannington—who were standing against the lockers watching me hand out clues. They didn't realize she was behind them, and she happened to overhear Arlene say sarcastically, "She's like some special kind of moron"—meaning me, I guess.

"I know," The Shadow agreed . . . then Kimberly said that Marcy added kind of wistfully, "But I sorta wish there *was* a way to get the extra curricular stuff back."

According to Kimberly, you would have thought Marcy was suggesting high acts of treason! Arlene turned one of her famous withering looks on Marcy and said, "Marcy! When are you going to stop thinking of yourself?" Then she stalked off, leaving her friend behind.

Poor Marcy. Kimberly said the girl just stood

there with an odd look on her face, as if she was thinking, "Wait a minute . . . there's something wrong with that statement."

Anyway. We passed out at least two hundred sheets listing the Code-Buster clues. That's a lot of brain power working together on this!

—Oh! Here come Matt and Rebecca. Gotta cut out, E.D. I promised they could help try to bust this code when they got here after school today. It's the final day and the final clue.

Over and out . . . and wish us luck!

— *Click!* —

It's over, E.D. . . . done . . . finished . . . terminated . . . the end . . .

I'm supposed to be in bed, but I just can't sleep. My old Teddy and I are sitting here on my window seat, trying to figure out what happened! *Sigh.* Maybe it would help to talk through what took place after the kids got here . . . so here goes . . .

Okay. Rebecca had the great idea of representing each clue with a real prop, to see if that would give us any ideas. So we gathered a toy FIRETRUCK . . . a small globe (to represent the word PLANET) . . . Dad's SAW . . . Mom's GUITAR . . . a BANANA (that one was easy) . . . a cheerleader's POM-POM I made out of crepe paper . . . even a stuffed ARMADILLO from one of Rebecca's friends!

Then I wrote all the clues on separate strips of

paper and stuck them on the refrigerator with magnets, so we could move the words all around in different combinations. We tried making a sentence out of the words, but there was one major problem . . . no verbs.

And there was still one clue missing! We turned the radio on and the WWEN deejay kept saying between songs, "All you would-be Code-Busters out there . . . stay tuned for the *final clue* . . . but first . . . blah, blah, blah."

Several times I felt hopeless. I was never going to break this code! But . . . then I remembered how many kids from school were listening to their radios right at that moment—like George and Bobby and Kimberly and, yeah, Cristan, and a lot of other dudes—waiting for the final clue, ready to pounce on the telephone. So then I'd feel hopeful once more . . . with so many kids working together, somebody was sure to solve it!

Matt, Rebecca, and I were moving our props around on the kitchen table, studying them, when the back door opened and Grandpa came in . . . and boy, did he look spiffed up! He was wearing a white shirt, vest, and bow tie . . . although he *did* have his shirt sleeves rolled up . . . and a strange man was with him.

"Hello, kids!" Grandpa said, beaming like a megawatt lightbulb. "This is an old high school buddy of mine . . . Wellington Riter."

Wellington Riter. What a distinguished name! And Grandpa's friend looked pretty distinguished, too, with his tan face and thin, gray moustache . . . but then he spoiled it all by bursting out laughing and saying, "Just call me Duke!"

I decided then and there that I liked Grandpa's friend.

"This is my granddaughter, Drea," Grandpa went on, giving me a hug, "and these are the two scalawags she baby-sits: Rebecca and Matt."

We all said "Hi" as Duke came over to the kitchen table, eyeing our pile of props with a quizzical look on his face.

"We're trying to win a R-A-D-I-O contest!" Matt explained, showing off his newest spelling word.

"Yeah," Rebecca chimed in, "we're gonna win so Drea can donate ten thousand dollars to her school so they can get all the good stuff back."

"Win? Ten thousand dollars?" said Duke, surprised. "Whew! That's a lot of money . . . what's all this 'good stuff' you're talking about?"

"Drama club, cheerleading, field trips, buses for away soccer games . . . you know, the *good* stuff!" I explained.

"Ah," said Duke, nodding seriously. "What happened?"

I didn't really want to explain it all, but he seemed genuinely interested, so I said, "Well, the school board zapped the funding—"

"This is it!" Rebecca interrupted, turning up the radio. "This is the final clue! Everybody be quiet!"

We all crowded around the radio—Matt, Rebecca, Grandpa, Duke, and me—practically holding our breaths as the Code-Buster theme music swelled up, and then . . .

"You're listening to Hampton Falls' hottest music on . . . Power Ten-Forty!" hyped the deejay. "All right, fans . . . are you ready to play . . . *CODE-BUSTER*?"

I leaned closer to the radio, pencil and paper ready.

"We've got ten thousand dollars for the *first* Code-Buster with the correct answer after our song ends," said the deejay. "And here's our last clue . . . CABOOSE."

I wrote it down quickly: CABOOSE.

As the music started, I realized that this was it—our last chance to crack the code! I tried to concentrate on the list of eight words on my pad of paper, and was only vaguely aware of Rebecca putting the new word up on the refrigerator.

I saw Grandpa whisper something to Matt, and Matt ran upstairs. While he was gone Grandpa printed the telephone number of the radio station in big numbers and stuck it by the phone. A few minutes later Matt came downstairs with the caboose from my dad's old train set—which he found up in the attic—to add to our props on the table.

Even Duke got caught up in the excitment. He sat down at the kitchen table, chewing on the end of his pencil as he played around with the code words on a piece of paper. Once he jumped up, thinking he had an idea . . . but when he showed us his paper, I saw that he had forgotten to write down the word POM-POM as one of the clues. So he shrugged, scratched his head, and sat down to think some more.

The tension was getting to me . . . everybody was working so hard . . . why couldn't we break the code?!

The tension must have been getting to Matt, too . . . 'cause once I looked up and he was eating the banana! As I rescued the half-eaten clue, I caught Duke's eye, and it was all we could do to keep from laughing.

Grandpa kept pacing up and down the kitchen, thinking, and at one point Duke went over to him. I know he thought he was whispering, but he must be a little hard of hearing 'cause I heard him say, "She's a pistol, Ben . . . I wish my grandkids had enough guts to try something as cockamamie as this."

Grandpa chuckled. "Remember when we thought nothing was impossible?"

"Yeah," Duke grinned, "that was a long time ago . . . before families and careers . . . ah! Those were great days, weren't they?"

"Some of the best!" Grandpa agreed, giving Duke's shoulder a squeeze.

Just then the back door opened and Mom and Dad both came in, kinda out of breath.

"Hi!" Mom said, shrugging off her suit jacket. "We heard the last clue in the car on the way home . . ."

"All the kids at the college are going nuts trying to solve this thing!" Dad exclaimed.

Oh, great, I thought. *Just what I wanted to hear . . . competition.*

Then my parents saw Grandpa's friend. "Oh, hi, Duke!" Dad said. "Having fun playing Code-Buster?"

"Oh, sure!" laughed Duke. "But this one's a dilly . . . it's got all of us stumped.

"It's probably right in front of our faces," said Rebecca.

I turned and looked at her. "Hmm," I said. "Right in front of our faces . . . maybe you're right, Rebecca. Maybe we're trying too hard! It's probably something obvious, like . . . like . . ."

I looked at the pile of props on the kitchen table and picked up the caboose.

"Like . . . since *caboose* is the *last* clue . . . and since a caboose is the *last* car on a train," I said, thinking out loud, ". . . maybe the code word has something to do with the *last* letter of every word . . ."

"Good thinking, Drea!" exclaimed Grandpa.

I looked at the last letters of the words scrambled on the refrigerator . . . K-A-T-E-W-O-R-M . . . well, that obviously wasn't it, but what . . . ?

I really didn't want to blow it . . . or a certain person with the initials A.B. would make me the laughing stock of Hampton Falls. As I stood there frantically thinking, my glance fell on a pair of salt and pepper shakers sitting on the counter . . .

. . . in a blink the pepper shaker top morphed into the face of Arlene Blake, her perfect hair done up under a gray, rounded beret, and she was laughing . . . LAUGHING at me . . . sitting there in my own kitchen, watching me spin my brain, laughing . . .

"Get out of my brain, Arlene Blake," I hissed, shaking my head to rid my imagination of the laughing pepper shaker. "Just because *you* don't want to work together on this . . ."

And then . . . it came to me.

"Wait a minute . . . wait a minute," I cried, grabbing my pad of paper again . . .

"C'mon, Drea!" yelled a gravelly voice. I knew without even looking up that my friend Mr. Toaster was doing a little tap dance on the kitchen counter.

114

"You can do it!" he cheered . . .

"Yes!" I said, jumping up. "I've got it! I've got it!"

"Hooray!" yelled Matt.

"Atta girl!" said Grandpa.

"Dial it! Dial it!" cried Rebecca.

I punched in the numbers Grandpa had put up right by the phone. "It's ringing . . . it's ringing!" I said excitedly to everyone, giving a quick glance at the kitchen counter . . .

The pepper shaker morphed again into Arlene's face . . . but this time Arlene's jaw had dropped in shock. "No!" she cried. "Tell me this isn't happening!"

"It's happening . . . it's happening!" crowed Mr. Toaster, giving the pepper shaker a little bump with his handle as he tapped away on the counter. "That's my Drea . . . I knew she could do it!" . . .

As the phone rang on the other end, each second seemed like an eternity. I had it! I knew it! I had solved the Code-Buster!

"What's the answer?" asked Matt, hopping up and down, trying to see my paper.

"C'mon, Drea!" cried Duke, excitedly punching Grandpa on the arm just like a kid.

Rebecca turned up the radio . . . Matt closed his eyes and crossed his fingers, wishing hard . . . and then we heard the deejay answer . . .

"You're the first caller," said the deejay's voice on the radio. "What's your answer?"

"'TEAMWORK'?" said a voice.

"Yes!" I yelled. "That's my answer!"

"Yes!" yelled the deejay. "You have just won ten thousand dollars!!"

Then it hit me with a SMASH. That wasn't my voice on the radio!

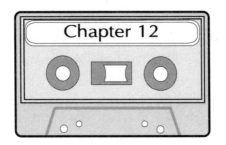

Defeat Defeated

"NO!" I cried. "That's *my* answer!"

But on the radio a young man's voice was saying, "Are you kidding me? I won? . . . Hey, guys! I won . . . I won!"

I can't even describe how I felt, E.D. . . . seeing the smiles fade on all those excited faces around me in the kitchen . . . being *this close* to getting that ten thousand dollars, and then . . . missing by a phone call . . . one lousy phone call . . .

Someone turned off the radio. All I could do was slump into a kitchen chair. "I don't believe this," I whispered. "I had it . . . I really had it . . ."

I put my pad of paper on the table. There it was in bold letters . . .

Sigh. I don't know when everybody left, E.D. . . . I don't even remember if I said good-bye to Grandpa and Duke. All I could think was that it's just not fair—

Oh . . . hi, Mom . . . yeah, come on in. I was just filling in my electronic diary on the Defeat of the Century . . .

— *Click!* —

Sorry for the interruption, E.D. I guess Mom heard me talking to myself up here and wondered if I was okay.

She came in and just sat on my window seat with me for a few minutes, not saying anything. Then . . . I couldn't help it . . . all the feelings just seemed to well up and spill out.

"Mom," I said, trying to swallow the lump that wanted to stick in my throat, "I was *so close.* Just think of all the good stuff that coulda happened."

And then Mom said a funny thing: "Right now I'm too busy thinking about what an amazing daughter I have."

"Amazing?" I said, not knowing whether to laugh or cry. "Get real, Mom. What's so amazing about losing?"

Mom looked out at the zillions of stars framed by my dormer window. "Well," she said, "how about a seventh grader who was able to crack that code? Or . . . how about, the only reason she wanted to win was to help her school?"

Then Mom reached out, took me in her arms, and we just sat there cuddled up on the window seat like we used to when I was little. "Oh, Sweetheart," she said, her breath warm on my hair, "I'm so proud of you!"

And as we sat there like that, the disappointment began to hurt just a little less, E.D.

But then I decided I better confess something.

"Of course . . . I *was* gonna keep the two Multiplex Theater passes," I admitted.

She laughed and just gave me another big hug before she went to bed . . . which is what I better do now, too, E.D. After all, it is a school day tomorrow.

But I have to admit . . . what I dread most is Arlene Blake *enjoying* my defeat.

— *Click!* —

It's Day 4,886 in the amazing Secret Adventures of Drea Thomas . . . and I do mean *amazing*, E.D.! I hardly know where to begin!

Okay, okay . . . it's Wednesday, the day after the Code-Buster Contest Disaster. Right now, it's almost seventeen-hundred hours—I mean, five o'clock—and Rebecca and Matt and I are waiting for their mom to get here, because we're all going to—

Wait. I'm already getting ahead of myself!

Back to the beginning. Are you ready for this, E.D.?

Okay . . . when I got to school, there was George sitting in the hallway under the goal poster I made, still trying to sell those horrible hoagies. It was pathetic . . . on the sign saying "Hoagies—$5.00," the five dollars had been crossed out . . . then $3.50, which was also crossed out . . . then $2.50, which was *also* crossed out . . . and finally scrawled at the bottom were the words, "Make Offer."

Kimberly and Bobby soon drifted in and joined George and me at the Hoagie table . . . I guess misery loves company.

"Anybody have the official results of our 'Save the E.C.A.'s' campaign?" Kimberly asked—but without her usual enthusiasm.

I shook my head. "Unchanged since our committee last met . . . Operation Win Big bit the dust along with all my favorite things to do around here."

Bobby picked up one of the leftover hoagies and looked at it from several angles. "There's still a chance we could sell the mold on the hoagies for medical research," he said sarcastically.

George grabbed the hoagie. "That's the *lettuce*, Bobby," he said.

At that moment, who should come walking down the hall but Arlene Blake, wearing that pink brocade jacket thing, with Marcy Mannington in tow, wearing a suitably mousy-colored top so she didn't outshine Arlene. I was hoping that Arlene would just ignore us and pass on by . . . but that was like expecting a bunch of girls at a slumber party to actually slumber.

Arlene batted her eyes and poured it on thick. "Well, Drea," she said, her voice dripping with sarcasm, "I'm *so sorry* to hear about that radio station thing . . . I heard you were this close." And she waved her hand vaguely.

"Hello, girls!" boomed a familiar masculine voice.

I looked up . . . and there was Grandpa's old high school friend walking toward us with the principal, Mrs. Long.

"What are you doing here, Duke?" I asked, surprised.

"What are you doing here, Grandfather?" Arlene asked at the exact same moment.

" '*Grandfather*'?!" Kimberly and I said together, staring incredulously at Arlene.

" '*Duke*'?!" Arlene and Marcy said together, their jaws hanging open.

But Duke didn't seem to notice we were all in shock.

"Well," he beamed, "I wanted to give Drea something before I went back to New York." He handed me a pretty gift bag with handles. "It's kind of a way of showing my appreciation."

I didn't have the faintest idea what he was talking about, but I opened the gift bag, reached in . . . and pulled out a snazzy-looking phone.

Arlene looked like she was going to have heart failure. "A phone!" she gasped. "You're giving her a *phone*?"

"He's giving her a phone?" Marcy echoed . . . but she backed off when Arlene glared at her.

"Yep!" Duke said, stabbing his finger at the phone. "It's got speed-dialing." He leaned close to me. "You shoulda won!"

I was completely flabbergasted. Here was Grandpa's best buddy from high school . . . who also happened to be the grandfather of my worst enemy . . . giving me a present in the hallway of Hampton Falls Junior High . . . and telling everybody *I* shoulda won the Code-Buster Contest. I mean, it was like he really believed in me!

But that's not all, E.D.

Duke—I mean, Mr. Riter—put his arm around me and said, "Drea, when your grandfather invited me over to your house, and you and those two scalawags you baby-sit for were working so hard to bust that code . . . and then we all got involved— your grandpa Ben and me and your mom and dad— I rediscovered how much fun it is to be part of a group that is pulling together."

Yeah, I thought, looking around at Kimberly and George and Bobby, who had been working hard, too, for our common goal. *It HAS been great working together . . . even if we're having to admit defeat.* I looked at my friends with new appreciation . . . then realized Duke was still talking.

"—figured I'd do my part to help 'zap' your problem," he was saying. "So . . ." he said, reaching inside his coat and pulling out a piece of paper, "I've drafted a check for ten thousand dollars to Hampton Falls Junior High to help cover your E.C.A. budget."

And with a little bow, he presented the check to Mrs. Long.

I blinked, speechless. I wanted to say something profound . . . heartfelt . . . impressive . . . important . . . to express what I was feeling.

"WOW!!" I said . . . and all I could see were big, fat, green dollar signs dancing around in front of my eyes.

But Mrs. Long came through. "Oh, Mr. Riter," she said, holding the check with delight, "this is so generous! How can we ever thank you?"

Duke chuckled. Now, I don't know Mr. Riter very well, E.D., but if my Grandpa Ben chuckled like that, I woulda been immediately suspicious that he had something up his sleeve.

Shoulda trusted my instinct . . . 'cause Duke said, "Well, Mrs. Long, there *is* a way . . ." And before I knew what was happening, Duke had put an arm around Arlene, and another arm around me, and he drew us together until we were practically nose to nose. "Next year," he announced, "I will match dollar for dollar everything that these two girls can raise . . . together."

"Together?!" said Arlene, in a tone of voice that implied she would rather be forced to eat green worms. "Grandfather, you have no idea what you're asking . . . it's impossible!"

But Duke just grinned. "Honey, nothing's impossible when you work together—"

Just then Duke's watch alarm went off.

"Ah! Time to go . . . got a plane to catch," he said. But then he whispered in Arlene's ear—which wasn't hard to hear since Duke had me clutched in his other arm— "Work with Drea, Honey . . . you'd make a great team."

Duke finally let both of us go. "See you later, Sweetie," he said, kissing Arlene's forehead. Then he turned to me and punched the air. "Code-Buster!"

As Duke walked out the front doors, the hallway seemed to erupt.

"We did it!" yelled Kimberly and George and Bobby, giving each other high fives . . . and then Kimberly grabbed the red marker and drew a long red line straight up the goal poster, clear to the very top.

"Pretty amazing, Drea!" said Mrs. Long, smiling and shaking her head. "You did it . . . I thought that it was impossible, but . . . you did it!"

It didn't take long for other kids in the hallway to figure out what was happening. "We got the E.C.A.'s back!" . . . "Hooray!" . . . "All right!" they yelled.

I was speechless . . . but I heard Marcy say to Arlene, "Drea just got *ten thousand dollars* from your grandfather . . . she's incredible!"

Just then the mob in the hallway kinda swept me away in their victory celebration. I looked back at Arlene, who was shooting daggers at me with her eyes and saying something. I couldn't hear the words, but I could definitely read her lips . . .

"I hate you, Drea Thomas!"

Which makes me wonder if Duke will *ever* get

his chance to "match dollar for dollar" anything Arlene and I can raise together next year for the E.C.A. budget, but . . . oh, well. Guess I'll cross that bridge when we get to it.

Anyway . . . at noon I called Mom at Jamison's Department Store, and then I called Dad at the college, to tell them both the good news . . . and guess what! I've been so wrapped up in my own problems, that I totally blanked out that *tonight* is Dad's "Sixty Minuets with Wolfie Mozart" concert!

But when Dad heard that we were gonna get our E.C.A.'s back, he offered to take us all out to a fancy dinner and then to the concert to celebrate! By "all" I mean our family—including Grandpa—plus Rebecca, Matt, and Mrs. Long! The kids are really excited to get dressed up and go to a real Mozart concert . . . but their mother had better get here soon, or she'll have to pick them off the wall first!

I'm excited, too . . . it'll be fun to go out to dinner with the Longs. I just wonder if Mrs. Long is prepared to be seen in a fancy restaurant with a man in a white powdered wig, a ruffled shirt, knee-breeches, and buckle shoes!

— *Click!* —

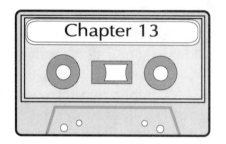

Chapter 13

Operation Cooperation

Saturday, Day 4,889 . . . Time: twelve-hundred hours . . . Place: back porch steps, where I'm soaking up some rays. I'm just taking a break while Grandpa bags up some of the leaves that thoughtlessly fell in our yard the last couple of weeks.

But before too many days go by, I wanted to say that our celebration dinner and the Sixty Minuets concert on Wednesday were a great success, E.D.! It was fun to see Rebecca and Matt and Mrs. Long all dressed up . . . although Matt tried to wear his blue and red baseball cap with his dress shirt and bow tie, much to Rebecca's disgust.

Yes, Dad did wear his "Wolfie Mozart" costume to the restaurant, and it caused quite a stir. Matt and Rebecca kept giggling at all the people who were staring at us . . . and several people came by our table to ask what was going on. So, Dad told them about Mozart's music . . . and I think I saw some of them later at the concert!

Dad's idea for publicizing the concert must've worked, 'cause the college concert hall was packed out. And Dad looked fantastic conducting the orchestra dressed like Wolfgang himself. The college administration hasn't said for sure, but personally, I think they'd be crazy to cancel future concerts after such a great—

Oh . . . sorry, Grandpa. What did you say?

— *Click!* —

Gotta go, E.D. I mean, Grandpa isn't exactly subtle. He's standing there in his plaid flannel shirt, holding a rake in one hand and a bag of leaves in the other . . . just waiting for me.

A moment ago he said to me philosophically, "You know, it really is amazing what can be done when everyone pulls together . . ."

I looked across the yard at him and called, "That must be my cue to get off my duff and help . . . right?"

Grandpa's face lit up with a big grin. "Right! You've learned this lesson well, Drea."

I wanted to take a little more time to finish this entry, but frankly, E.D., I haven't yet figured out how to hold a rake in both hands *and* talk into my Walkman at the same time. So . . . it's back to Operation Cooperation . . . hey! That would be a good name for our campaign to "Save the E.C.A.'s" . . . next year!

Anyway, this is Drea Thomas, signing off before I drop this thing. After all we've gone through together, E.D., I don't want my electronic diary to be gone in a SMASH.

— Click! —

Telling Time the
SECRET ADVENTURES Way!

Use the following chart to tell time like Drea's Mighty Morphing Watch!

(*Note:* "Military time" is based on a 24-hour day—unlike "civilian time," which is based on two 12-hour time periods).

12-hour clock   *24-hour clock*

1 o'clock a.m.   *0100 hours (oh-one-hundred hours)*
2 o'clock a.m.   *0200 hours (oh-two-hundred hours)*
3 o'clock a.m.   *0300 hours (oh-three-hundred hours)*
4 o'clock a.m.   *0400 hours (oh-four-hundred hours)*
5 o'clock a.m.   *0500 hours (oh-five-hundred hours)*

6 o'clock a.m.	0600 hours (oh-six-hundred hours)
7 o'clock a.m.	0700 hours (oh-seven-hundred hours)
8 o'clock a.m.	0800 hours (oh-eight-hundred hours)
9 o'clock a.m.	0900 hours (oh-nine-hundred hours)
10 o'clock a.m.	1000 hours (ten-hundred hours)
11 o'clock a.m.	1100 hours (eleven-hundred hours)
12 o'clock p.m.	1200 hours (twelve-hundred hours)

Watch out! Here's where it gets tricky!

1 o'clock p.m.	1300 hours (thirteen-hundred hours)
2 o'clock p.m.	1400 hours (fourteen-hundred hours)
3 o'clock p.m.	1500 hours (fifteen-hundred hours)
4 o'clock p.m.	1600 hours (sixteen-hundred hours)
5 o'clock p.m.	1700 hours (seventeen-hundred hours)
6 o'clock p.m.	1800 hours (eighteen-hundred hours)
7 o'clock p.m.	1900 hours (nineteen-hundred hours)
8 o'clock p.m.	2000 hours (twenty-hundred hours)
9 o'clock p.m.	2100 hours (twenty-one-hundred hours)
10 o'clock p.m.	2200 hours (twenty-two-hundred hours)
11 o'clock p.m.	2300 hours (twenty-three-hundred hours)
12 o'clock a.m.	2400 hours (twenty-four-hundred hours)

Minutes in between hours are described like this:

10:15 a.m.	1015 hours (ten-fifteen hundred hours)
6:30 p.m.	1830 hours (eighteen-thirty hundred hours)

In everyday speech, the words "hours" or "hundred hours" are often dropped. (E.g., "Meet me at school at oh-eight-hundred, okay?" "Be home for chow at eighteen-thirty—sharp!")

DAY
4,134

Figure Your Age the
Secret Adventures Way

Want to know how many days old you are?
Here's how . . .
1. Multiply your age by 365 days. (For example:
   There are 365 days in each year. If you are 11
   years old, multiply 365 x 11 = 4,015.)
2. Next, add one day for every "leap year"
   you've been alive. (Note: every fourth year has
   an extra day in February, or 366 days, which is

called leap year.) Here are some current leap years: 1980, 1984, 1988, 1992, 1996, 2000.

3. Now get a calendar (you may need last year's calendar, too, if you haven't had your birthday yet this year) and count how many days it's been since your LAST birthday until TODAY.

4. Add your totals from Steps 1, 2, and 3. (For example: 4,015, plus 3 leap years ['84, '88, and '92], plus, say, 116 days since your last birthday = today would be Day 4,134 in the Secret Adventures of You!)

LOOK FOR THIS HOT VIDEO RELEASE FROM BROADMAN & HOLMAN GUEST STARRING MICHAEL W. SMITH.

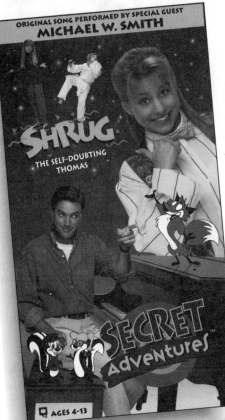